Letters to an American Christian is a substantive. wid~.
ranging, often-funny treatise on ~~
the United States. Ashford doesn
most intractable problems or fi
writes with winsomeness and (
ward for those who may feel poli~~ ~~ ~~... uays.
Even if you don't agree with his take on every issue, you'll
find yourself thinking (and chuckling) all the way through
this brilliant book.

> **Trevin Wax**, Bible and reference publisher at
> LifeWay Christian Resources, author of *Eschatological
> Discipleship: Leading Christians to Understand Their
> Historical and Cultural Context* and *This Is Our Time:
> Everyday Myths in Light of the Gospel*

Religion and politics are two of the most difficult topics for
Americans to discuss today. Too often they generate more
heat than light. *Letters to an American Christian* is different.
Bruce Ashford has produced a highly readable and eminently
sensible series of reflections on faith and public life. It's a
book American Christians need now.

> **Ryan T. Anderson**, author of *Truth Overruled:
> The Future of Marriage and Religious Freedom*
> and *When Harry Became Sally:
> Responding to the Transgender Moment*

A fantastic, enlightening, and entertaining analysis that perfectly reads the zeitgeist and offers humble, practical, and
biblically faithful counsel.

> **J.D. Greear**, lead pastor of
> The Summit Church (Raleigh-Durham)

Bruce Ashford has shown the way for Christian political conservatives to navigate in this post-Christian world. He illustrates that we need not be locked into a culture war approach

nor head for the hills. His smart, informed and insightful advice should be heeded by Christian conservatives in the coming years. You need to buy *Letters to an American Christian*. No, buy two and give one to a friend.

George Yancey, professor of Sociology,
University of North Texas

Bruce Ashford brings much-needed clarity, consistency, and conviction to a range of concerns swirling amidst the sea of moral confusion that surrounds the church and the culture today. Every Christian will benefit from reading *Letters to an American Christian*.

Karen Swallow Prior, author of *On Reading Well: Finding the Good Life through Great Books*

With the decline of civics education in the United States, we need to find new and creative ways to help students think about politics. Bruce Ashford has written a book that I think young Christians will find accessible, compassionate, current, and careful. I don't know another theologian who could write a book about politics that is so well-calibrated for Christians of Generation Z.

Hunter Baker, JD, PhD, University Fellow for
Religious Liberty, Union University

The American political landscape is an increasingly difficult space for Christians to navigate. Ashford offers a vision for Christian political engagement and applies it to the most pressing issues of the day. *Letters to an American Christian* is required reading for believers who desire to reflect biblical faith in the public square.

Walter Strickland, assistant professor of
Systematic and Contextual Theology,
Southeastern Baptist Theological Seminary

LETTERS

TO AN

AMERICAN

CHRISTIAN

LETTERS

TO AN

AMERICAN

CHRISTIAN

BRUCE RILEY ASHFORD

PUBLISHING GROUP

NASHVILLE, TENNESSEE

978-1-5359-0513-8

Published by B&H Publishing Group
Nashville, Tennessee

Dewey Decimal Classification: 261.7
Subject Heading: CHRISTIANITY AND POLITICS \
CITIZENSHIP \ AMERICANS

1 2 3 4 5 6 7 ▪ 22 21 20 19 18

To my children—Riley, Anna Kate, and Kuyper—without whose constant encouragement and ceaseless conversation this book would have been completed in half the time.

ACKNOWLEDGMENTS

Most of this book was written early in the mornings, and I would like to acknowledge the Main Street Grille (Wake Forest, North Carolina), whose apple cider doughnuts made the task of writing at 6:00 a.m. such an enjoyable exercise.

I wish to thank Devin Maddox and Taylor Combs at B&H Publishing Group for their commitment to this project and the Kern Family Foundation, whose encouragement and support enabled this project to become a reality. I am also grateful for those persons who, through critical feedback, research, editing, and proofreading, made this manuscript better than it would have been: Hunter Baker for his critical feedback on several chapters; Joe Carter for his research for chapters 10, 12, 13, 18, and 23; Dennis Greeson for his research for chapters 11 and 15; Chris Pappalardo for editing the manuscript; Chris Martin for his encouragement and counsel; and Cindy Hotchkiss and Jackie Sanderlin, who assisted in preparing the manuscript for submission. I am thankful for good friends and colleagues who have sharpened my thinking, including but not limited to political scientists David Koyzis and Hunter Baker, ethicist Daniel Heimbach, and public theologians Craig Bartholomew and Jonathan Leeman.

I thank several media outlets for allowing me to repurpose content originally written for them: Daily Signal for content related to chapters 9 and 22; Daily Caller for content related to chapters 14 and 19; and Fox News Opinion for content related to chapter 14.

And finally, I express my love and appreciation for my wife Lauren, who has been my partner in thinking and writing since 2007.

CONTENTS

PART 1

A CHRISTIAN VIEW
OF POLITICS AND
PUBLIC LIFE

CHAPTER 1

NO PUBLIC NUDITY, PLEASE

Dear Christian,

Thank you for writing. I'm excited to hear that you've recently become a Christian. I mean, considering your name and all, it seems *apropos*. I'm especially happy you took the time to inquire about how your Christian faith should affect your political views. I'm a political junkie too, and just like you, when I became a Christian, I had to think about how my political views would be affected by my faith.

You made me laugh when you said that the 2016 election cycle felt like a "never-ending carnival of political wedgies." I couldn't have put it better myself. It bothered me that, from the primary debates onward, the whole thing seemed like a combination of a war, a carnival, and a Hollywood movie (and the worst aspects of all three!). Like you, I wish there had been more of a serious and reasoned debate. In a time like ours, a few eulogies for political civility would not be out of place.

I think the most important question you asked in your letter is whether religion and politics should be mixed at all. As you mentioned, your professor at Dupont University argued that the two should never be mixed, but many of the Christians you know think the two mix quite well. If I'm reading the subtext of your letter rightly, you don't seem particularly impressed with either answer.

Let me start by saying that your professor at Dupont isn't alone in his view. Many Americans agree with Thomas Haliburton when he said, "Never discuss religion or politics with those who hold opinions opposite to yours; they are subjects that heat in handling, until they burn your fingers."[1] Let's face it: if we bring up religion and politics in a social situation, things can get heated pretty quickly.

But it's not just awkwardness that keeps many Americans from wanting to mix politics and religion; they think it makes us better citizens if we lay aside our religious beliefs when determining what is just and unjust.

The most famous contemporary proponent of this view is a Harvard political philosopher named John Rawls. Rawls argued that Americans citizens hide behind a "veil of ignorance" when trying to come to grips with public justice.[2] Additionally he argued that public debate should be conducted without reference to the types of "comprehensive doctrines" found in world religions or ideologies such as Marxism.[3]

Many Americans are less nuanced than Rawls and go further than he does. They argue that when we engage in public debate about political matters, we should pretend that we are not aware of our own religious commitments, political ideologies, race, social class, or economic status. Ideas should battle ideas, regardless of who is making them.

The first problem with this flawed view is that it assumes American citizens can—and should—separate their public "self" from their private "self." It assumes we could be as religious as we want when we are at home or at church but could just as easily become nonreligious when we enter into public discussion and debate. In other words, Rawls views religion like clothing: we can put it on and take it off at will.

Those who hold this view usually have good intentions, I imagine. They want Americans to seek good political solutions for *all* of their fellow citizens, rather than engaging in politics that seek good deals only for people who share their religion, race, economic level, or social status. The goal, in other words, is ethical and equitable politics. Yet despite good intentions this proposed solution won't work. I seem to remember a saying about where roads paved with good intentions alone lead us . . .

This approach won't work for three big reasons. First, *human beings are deeply and inescapably religious.* We cannot *not* be religious. Now I know that many people consider themselves atheist or agnostic, but that doesn't mean they've somehow become religion-free. "Religion" is not a category that should be restricted to those persons who worship a supernatural deity. Most Buddhists, for example, would describe themselves as "religious," but many of them do not worship a supernatural deity.

That is why the Bible considers religion in terms of "ultimate commitments." All human beings commit themselves to somebody or something in an ultimate way. All human beings have somebody or something to which they give their highest trust and love. That someone might be the God of Jesus Christ or the Allah of Muhammad. Alternatively, it might be something less obviously religious in appearance, like sex, money, power, or success. Regardless, that somebody or something sits on the throne of their hearts, commanding their loyalties, shaping their lives, and offering some sort of respite from life's pains and evils. The center cannot remain empty. It's been said that nature abhors a vacuum; the heart does too.

This brings us to our second point. Precisely because religion involves our ultimate commitments, *we cannot separate our public self from our private self.* If religion were merely the mental and mystical acknowledgment of a supernatural deity, we could easily relegate that belief to the confines of our private lives and to certain religious ceremonies. But religion is not a matter of private worship we can keep bottled up. As the Bible defines it, religion is the central organizer of a person's thoughts and loves.

By locating religion in the human "heart," the Bible hints that religion affects us in the deepest aspects of who we are and radiates outward into everything we do. If a person really and truly embraces the God of Jesus as the Creator and Lord of the universe, that embrace will have a cascade effect, pouring down and out into that person's beliefs, feelings, values, and actions. Similarly, if a person absolutizes sex or money or power, that absolutization will cascade outward from the private recesses to the public words and actions of that person. Many Americans hear this and get angry that I'm saying we *shouldn't* keep religion private. But in fact, I'm saying something far more radical: human beings *can't.*

For Christians, there is a third reason this flawed approach doesn't work: *Our Christian faith functions as the deepest motivation for contributing to the common good of our nation.* More than anything else the Bible's teaching and Jesus' example motivate us to want justice and equality for our fellow citizens (even when they are members of a different religion, race, or class). My Christian faith gives me the courage to criticize powerful politicians, corporations, or influencers even when there might be negative repercussions for doing so. Biblical teaching reminds me to remain civil during public discussion and debate even when my opponents misrepresent me or attack me. Take that part of me away, and you've taken away the best part.

To get back to your question at the beginning of the letter, the point is that religion and politics really can't be separated. As bright as Rawls and others are, they're wrong on this one. Religion is not like clothing that can be put on or taken off whenever we wish. It is less like a jacket or a pair of jeans and more like our heart. It is a part of who we are and cannot be removed on a whim. So, Christian, the point is this: don't try to get (religiously) naked in the public square.

As you mentioned in your letter, however, many Christians mix religion and politics in unhelpful ways. You're right. There are good and bad ways to mix politics. That is why we should study the Bible and the Christian tradition with a special focus on how to employ our religious convictions in ways that are politically helpful.

Consider, for example, the Bible's teaching that our words and actions should be characterized by truth *and* grace. If a Christian aims at truth but not grace, he will become little more than a loud-mouthed amateur lobbyist standing in the public square, sweating and yelling at passersby. (Have I described your Facebook wall for you?) If a Christian aims at grace but not at truth, she will become a sellout, sacrificing biblical convictions in order to avoid offending a society that has turned against Christian convictions. To put it differently, this combination of truth and grace should keep us from being either bullies or wimps in our political engagement.

That's just one example of how our Christian faith can positively influence our political views and public posture. There are others. Our faith should help us maintain a critical distance from any secular political ideology by providing us a vantage point from which to critique the negative aspects of that ideology. It should help us maintain a Christian demeanor in public debate, even when our debate partners might misrepresent us, mock us, or otherwise demean us. It will help us reframe public policy issues in ways that sometimes transcend the major party divide. I could go on, but hey, I've written too much already.

One last thing: toward the end of your letter, you mentioned the disillusionment you feel right now in relation to American politics. Believe me, I can relate. From where I sit, the past several years have put on full display the dysfunctional, mephitic, and effluvial travesty that is contemporary American politics. We have experienced the increasing disintegration of both major political parties; the superficiality, inanity, and pettiness often displayed by the candidates (and interviewers) in presidential debates; the inability of Congress to carry on a sustained or constructive debate on matters of grave national importance; the escalation of race-related crimes and unrest; a blatant disregard for the Constitution shown by the Supreme Court majority in some of its rulings; and the calloused and flippant attitudes of Planned Parenthood executive staffers when talking about taking the lives of unborn children and selling their dismembered body parts. The list could go on, *ad nauseum, ad infinitum.*

Yet, the times when we are the most disillusioned may turn out to be the times when it is most important for us to stay engaged. As G. K. Chesterton once wrote, "When you love a thing, its gladness is a reason for loving it, and its sadness a reason for loving it more."[4] Certainly these are sad times for American politics. But if we love our nation and our neighbors, this American sadness should only redouble our resolve. Our nation needs us. So let's put our Christian faith to work. Let's draw on its rich resources in order to help our nation.

Christian, thank you for writing. If you want to continue the conversation, let me know. The fact that you are studying political science and journalism at a left-leaning university such as Dupont but interning at a conservative news outlet makes your situation unique. As you mentioned, it's a disorienting combination. But it also means that you are well poised to leverage your Christianity to make a positive contribution to American politics.

Yours,
Bruce

CHAPTER 2

THE GOOD OF POLITICS

Christian,

I'm happy to hear from you again. I wasn't sure if you'd respond to my last letter at all, but you fired back quickly and thoughtfully. You made a number of good points and raised some fine questions, but the one thing that stood out the most to me is your question about whether or not a Christian should "waste his time" with politics. Your question reminds me of the great philosopher, Plato, who once quipped, "Those who are too smart to engage in politics are punished by being governed by those who are dumber." It also reminds me of Ronald Reagan, perhaps not so great a philosopher, but just as witty. Reagan once said, "Politics is supposed to be the second-oldest profession. I have come to realize that it bears a very close resemblance to the first."[1]

Plato and the Gipper are not alone. Many people view politics as a disreputable activity, undertaken by people they do not respect, fighting over policies they do not understand. And there is good evidence that something has gone badly wrong in the realm of politics. Even a person who possesses only the dimmest spark of critical reflectiveness can recognize that the political realm is plagued with all sorts of problems and problematic people.

But I think it is a big mistake to conclude that politics is inherently evil or a waste of time. In fact, Christians have good reasons to participate in government and politics. After all, the purpose of *government*, as I see it, is to do justice to the diversity of individuals and communities under its purview. The purpose of *politics* is to influence or oversee government policy. The purpose of *political engagement* is to persuade our fellow citizens and elected representatives toward the best view of justice and toward the best policies. Of course the Bible has something to say about these things!

Considering what the Bible has to say about politics can be tricky, especially if you're looking for specific verses. Those verses exist, but the better way to understand what the Bible teaches about politics is to trace its overarching story line. The Bible is not primarily a collection of religious truths or ethical principles but is rather a story best understood in four "acts"—creation, fall, redemption, and consummation. Believe it or not, each of these acts relates in one way or another to politics, so I'll take a few minutes to tell the story.

The Bible's opening act is creation. The Bible's first sentence declares, "In the beginning God created the heavens and the earth" (Gen. 1:1). It teaches us that God created matter from nothing, shaped that matter into the world as we now see it, and then—with a final flourish—created human beings in his "image" and "likeness" (Gen. 1:26). So human beings are the crown jewel of creation, at once unified with the rest of creation but also distinct from that creation.

Interestingly, God follows up immediately by giving the first couple, Adam and Eve, tasks that are social, cultural, and (if you'll forgive the mundane word) managerial. God instructs them to "be fruitful" and "multiply," a *social* task that involves making families and, by implication, societies (Gen. 1:28). He calls them to till the earth, a *cultural* task that involves bringing out the hidden potentials of God's creation. Finally, he tells them to "subdue it," a *managerial* task that involves acting in the world on God's behalf.

Now, before going on, I need to stop for a moment to talk about the cultural task. When God instructed the first couple to till the soil, he wasn't merely saying, "Hey, you guys should be farmers," though the farming metaphor is intentional and apt. He was saying something deeper and more profound. He was telling them to interact with the good world he had created, to make something out of what God had made, to bring out the world's hidden potentials. In other words, he was telling them to make culture. Farmers cultivate (same root word as *culture*) the physical earth to draw out plants; humans cultivate the created world to draw out its latent possibilities. We may not all be farmers, but we are all *culture farmers.*

One significant realm of culture is politics, and I think God intended human life to be characterized by government and politics all along. After all, he is the one who told human beings to make families and grow the human race, and any time large groups of humans live together, there is the need for government of some type. Now in those early days before there was any sin in the world, the government wouldn't have needed to have police officers, judges, or armies. Instead, government would have involved the ordering of human life. Somebody would need to decide which side of the road to drive on, which day to hold the Fall Festival, and so forth.

So, Christian, how does the creation act relate to your question? Here's how Chris Pappalardo and I put it in our book, *One Nation Under God*:

> Although we might be tempted to view politics as something not worth our time or beyond the pale of God's power, we need to remind ourselves that God created the type of world in which a collective ordering of society is necessary, and he remains sovereign over this world. He is sovereign over politics and, to the extent that we find ourselves involved in public life, we should consciously allow him to be sovereign over our involvement.[2]

The Bible's second act is the fall, and I find it fascinating. At the end of creation, the Bible depicts God's world as being characterized by love, order, peace, and justice. The first couple had a healthy and life-giving relationship with God, each other, and the world around them. God's intention was for humanity to live forever in this ideal state.

They wouldn't.

Sadly, the first couple chose a different path. You can read how it went down in Genesis 3. Adam and Eve turned against God and tried to enthrone themselves as king and queen of the world rather than being satisfied to manage the world under God's kingship. When they turned against God, everything began to unravel. Instead of an unbroken experience of love, order, peace, and justice, they would now also experience hatred, disorder, violence, and injustice. Instead of healthy and life-giving relationships, they would now experience brokenness and dysfunction in their relationships with God, each other, and the world around them. The result? Well, take a look at the world around you. Not a pretty picture, is it?

In fact, it's tempting to look at the evil in this world and conclude that this world is *inherently* bad. But the creation-fall narrative prevents you from making that kind of conclusion. Think of it this way: after the fall, the world remained structurally good but became directionally corrupt.[3]

Let me explain. When I say the world remained *structurally* good, I mean that the world was still structured the way God intended; human beings still had opportunity to be in right relationship to God, each other, and the world; they still had the privilege of fulfilling their social, cultural, and political callings; they still could participate in cultural activities such as art, agriculture, and politics.

Yet, even though the world remained structurally good, it became *directionally* bad. Human efforts were no longer directed toward God and toward the good God intended. Instead, human efforts were directed toward wrong and selfish ends, and those selfish ends corrupted their relationships and their cultural efforts.

So it should be no surprise that the realm of politics is twisted and corrupt. All of life is. We should not be shocked when people govern the world in ways that are unjust, unwise, or unloving. We should expect that citizens and their elected officials will be tempted to use power to serve themselves at the neglect of others. The problem is not that politics is an inherently bad realm of culture or that politicians are especially bad people (not always, anyway). No, the problem is that politics is like every other realm; it is populated by people who are constantly tempted to direct their efforts toward wrong and selfish ends.

Yet, thankfully, the Bible's story does not end with humanity's fall into corruption. The next act is redemption. Humanity descended quickly into sin and rebellion, but even more quickly God provided a way out of the mess.

Immediately after Adam and Eve sinned, God promised to send a Savior who would undo the curse of sin (Gen. 3:15). In fact, the majority of the Bible tells the fascinating series of developments that led to the coming of Jesus Christ, the Savior.

Here's how Chris and I put it in *One Nation under God*:

> What was a promise to Adam and Eve is a historical fact for us. God *did* come to earth in the person of Jesus Christ, proving how far he would come to recover his own. And Jesus *did* preach of a new kingdom, one in which God's peace, love, and flourishing would be restored. He *did* die on a cross as the sacrificial substitute for sinful humanity. He *did* step out of the grave three days later, forever settling the question of whether he would prevail.[4]

Christian, one of the things I liked most about your letter is the way you expressed gratitude for Jesus and the way he saved you from your sin and its consequences. But I want to challenge you to go a little bit further. Not only did he save you *from* something; he also saved you *for* something. He saved you for a newer and better life, a way of living directed toward God and the good he intends rather than toward selfish and bad ends. This new way of living will affect your whole life in its personal, social, cultural, and political dimensions. If you understand it in the right way, the redemption Jesus brings will never let you completely abandon politics.

The final act of the Bible, consummation, is really just an extension of the third act. The Bible promises that Jesus will return one day to complete what he started when he rose from the dead. Christian hope is our belief that Jesus will return one day to establish himself as King and will rule over a one-world government characterized by justice, peace, order, and love (Rev. 21–22). It is, in the words of John Milton, "paradise regained."

So, Christian, I hope I've been able to open your eyes to the enduring (albeit complicated) good of politics. It was created by God as a good and inescapable dimension of human life. Although human sin inevitably twists and corrupts human political efforts, we as Christians should allow our Christian faith to help untwist what has been twisted and bring healing to the corruption. Now the real question is *how* to untwist what has been twisted and how to bring healing to political corruption. That's the trick.

You mentioned that you will be taking six midterm exams this week. (My best recommendation is to set up an intravenous drip of Pike Place, OK?) If you make it out of this week alive, let me know, and we can continue the conversation.

Yours,

Bruce

CHAPTER 3

JESUS IS LORD AND CONGRESS IS NOT

Christian,

I can see that my last letter hasn't entirely convinced you. But first things first: congratulations on making it through midterms and for making an A+ on your foreign policy exam. That's no small task, especially considering the reading list your professor gave you. Having to know Henry Kissinger's *Diplomacy* cover to cover? That thing is nine hundred pages and probably weighs more than my dog. (I don't recommend reading *Diplomacy* in bed for fear that you would doze off and be crushed to death midsentence.)

Ostensibly you agree with me that politics is a God-given dimension of human life. You still wonder, however, whether Christians should ever prioritize it since "the gospel has little or nothing to do with politics." As one who previously said such things with frequency and conviction, I want to challenge you on that statement.

On the one hand, you are absolutely right that Jesus did not join a political party or run for political office. So in that sense he and his gospel are not political. But based on this, it is more accurate to say the gospel is not *exclusively* or *primarily* political. Because, on the other hand, Jesus' life and message were political in a much deeper and more profound sense.

Imagine walking out onto the quad where you overhear two of your friends talking. You know them fairly well, but you can't make sense of their conversation. One of your friends looks at the other and says, "And then we put a Coke in one hand and a cigar in the other!" while howling in laughter. The other friend joins in, wiping tears of laughter away from her eyes, "On the cafeteria roof! Bahahaha!"

You're not sure what happened with the Coke and the cafeteria roof, but you assume it's the punch line to a joke. Smiling, you walk up to them and say, "Sounds like a pretty funny joke, fellows. Why don't you let me in on it?" What they tell you, however, is that this is a real piece of recent history. Just yesterday, they inform you, they found a dead skunk on campus, which they decided to place on a perch atop the campus cafeteria's roof. They placed a ball cap on its head, a Dupont University T-shirt on its torso, a Coke in one hand, and a cigar in the other. All this happened just in time for a campus representative to bring a group of twenty prospective students around the corner, telling them, "Dupont University's cafeteria is not like ones you might find at other colleges." Indeed.

Why did you initially think your two friends were telling a joke when in fact they were recounting a recent prank? Well, because you walked into the middle of the conversation without knowing the context. But what happens when we walk into the middle of the story of Scripture, selecting some Bible verses about the gospel without knowing the context for those verses? The same thing will happen although the consequences are a bit more severe. We will not understand the gospel well if at all.

That is why we must place our conversations about the gospel in the context of the Bible's story, which I talked about in the last letter. Jesus was concerned with context and always took care to connect his own life and ministry to the Bible's story line. The apostle Paul did also. So let's talk about the word *gospel*.

When Jesus uses the word *gospel*, two types of context help us understand it. First, historical context. In Jesus' day, during the reign of the Roman Empire, *gospel* was a common term referring to the announcement of significant events. It wasn't a religious word. Usually, gospels were announcements of great things the emperor had done. But the Christian gospel was an announcement about somebody greater than the emperor—Jesus Christ; the Christian gospel was a challenge to the emperor because it was the happy news that Jesus is the true King of the world. The political leaders of Jesus' day rightly recognized that his ministry was a political threat—not a partisan threat but a political threat nonetheless.

Second, biblical context. Jesus' use of *gospel* reminded his listeners of the prophet Isaiah, who said, "How beautiful on the mountains are the feet of those who bring *good news* [that's "gospel"], who proclaim peace, who bring good tidings, who proclaim salvation, who say to Zion, 'Your God reigns!'" (Isa. 52:7 NIV).

The historical and biblical contexts combine to reveal a powerful truth: Jesus is the only King to whom all people and all of the world's leaders owe allegiance. And we, as Christians, should help our fellow citizens realize this and submit to Jesus' kingship over their lives.

Another way to think about this is to look at how Paul defines the gospel at the beginning of 1 Corinthians 15:

"Now I want to make clear for you, brothers and sisters, the gospel . . . that Christ died for our sins according to the Scriptures, that he was buried, that he was raised on the third day according to the Scriptures, and that he appeared to Cephas, then to the Twelve" (vv. 1, 3–5).

The Australian scholar John Dickson refers to this Bible passage as a five-point "bulleted summary" of the gospel.[1] I think he's right, and I think it applies to the relationship between the gospel and politics. These are his five points:

1.   Jesus is the Christ.
2.   Jesus died for our sins.
3.   Jesus was buried.
4.   Jesus rose from the dead.
5.   Jesus made public appearances.

First, Jesus is the Christ. "Christ" is not Jesus' last name, as if he had been born to Joseph and Mary Christ. No, "Christ" is a title that refers to Jesus being the King and Savior of the world. It encapsulates everything the Bible's four Gospels teach about Jesus, including his birth, teachings, and miracles. Paul starts this passage with "Christ" because he wants to remind us of Jesus' credentials as King. Political enough for you?

Second, Jesus died for our sins. The Bible also teaches that God loves us and does not want us to suffer the penalty of our sin. For that reason he took on a human body and came to earth as Jesus of Nazareth. When he did that, he "traded places" with us. He lived the sinless life we should have lived and died the death we deserve to die. He took our guilty record, died for it, and offers us his perfect record in return. That is why the apostle Paul declared that "there is now no condemnation for those in Christ Jesus" (Rom. 8:1).

Third, Jesus was buried. He really did die. He lay in a grave. Not in a bizarre, metaphorical way, but literally and historically. But *fourth, he rose from the dead!* The resurrection is the lead paragraph of the gospel news story. As one theologian put it, Jesus' resurrection wouldn't be in the "religion section" of the newspaper but would have been headline news. Jesus the King had not been defeated by death. Instead, he was raised from the dead, demonstrating his victory over sin, Satan, and death.

Fifth, he appeared publicly to many witnesses. His resurrection is not only publicly verified, but it is an event with public (and political!) ramifications. If it's true, then no aspect of life can remain the same.

From 1 Corinthians 15, we can see that the gospel is deeply and profoundly political. It is an announcement that Jesus is the Christ, the ultimate Ruler of the world, and all people should acknowledge him as such. The first political application of the gospel is that we, as American Christians, should hold our other political allegiances—to presidents, parties, and platforms—tentatively by comparison. We should continually evaluate our political stances, and our public words and actions, to bring them in line with his teachings.

We also notice that the gospel is a public truth. When Jesus died for our sins, he did so publicly. When he rose from the dead, he made public appearances to more than five hundred people. And if Jesus made public appearances to this many people after his resurrection, clearly the way we follow him has public ramifications as well.

The Bible compares the gospel both to a pearl and to leaven. The gospel is like a pearl because we treasure it in our hearts, and it is like leaven because it changes us in the totality of who we are. It sends us back into the world—socially, culturally, and politically—in a wholly new way. I've heard it said that God is like a spiritual cyclone: he draws us close to him only to quickly propel us back, with a mission, into our communities.

You see, people sometimes divide the world into two realms: the private and the public. They view Jesus as the spiritual ruler of their private lives and the government as the ruler of their public lives. Unfortunately, they even use Jesus' words to make this distinction. "Give to Caesar the things that are Caesar's, and to God the things that are God's" (Mark 12:13–17). But read that story a little closer. Jesus wasn't trying to say God owns our hearts while Caesar owns the rest. He was letting his listeners know that Caesar's rule was miniscule compared to God's. "Look at this coin," Jesus says, in effect. "It's got Caesar's mug on it—his image. So give him what he deserves. Pay your taxes. But whose image is on you? You were made in God's image, and he alone deserves your ultimate allegiance." The government can lay claim to some of our money, but only God can lay claim to our lives.

We've had a lot of good leaders who reminded us of this truth. One of the most prominent in recent history is Martin Luther King Jr. Dr. King's Christianity motivated him and gave him the worldview to speak and act against ungodly injustices being perpetrated against black Americans. But his proper respect for the government and for his fellow citizens caused him to lead like-minded citizens in *nonviolent* protests. He saw a political goal, and he acted on it within the political boundaries he was given. But both the power behind his protests and the law that limited his decisions came from the gospel. His life was an extended parable, proclaiming, "Jesus is Lord and our government is not."

Jesus is Lord. Caesar is not. Congress is not. The Democratic Party is not. The Republican Party is not. But Jesus' lordship has a confrontational and healing word for every "caesar" of every time. To the extent that we truly do acknowledge Jesus as Lord, we will engage the Caesar before us with compassion, respect, and wisdom, speaking and acting in ways that contribute to the common good. In other words, the more we pledge allegiance to Christ, the better citizens of the United States of America we'll become.

I suppose I've rambled on long enough for one letter. As Abraham Lincoln once said, "I could write shorter sermons, but once I start I get too lazy to stop."

I look forward to hearing from you soon.

Yours,

Bruce

CHAPTER 4

CHRISTIANITY IS NOT
OUR SIDE HUSTLE

Christian,

I'm glad you found my last couple of letters helpful. You didn't say it in so many words, but I'll assume for now that I've won you over when it comes to the connection between Christianity and politics.

You've asked me how I came to be interested in Christianity and politics. The short answer is, "by accident"—or, if you want to be picky, "by the providence of God." As for the longer answer . . .

My parents became Christians when I was very young. As I grew up, I recognized the sincerity of their faith and experienced the fruit of their faith. Their lives were genuinely shaped—reshaped, you might say—by the gospel. They read their Bibles, prayed, and showed genuine love to the people they encountered. They fought back against the racism that sometimes permeated the air in our small southern town. They gave sacrificially to our church and to the poor.

They were my first formative example of the Christian life, and I cannot overstate my debt to them.

As much as I learned about Christianity from my parents, however, I didn't get a clear picture of what Christianity had to do with the so-called "secular" aspects of life. Especially after I became a Christian myself, I wondered if Christianity applied to anything other than the most overtly religious activities. Did my newfound faith have anything to say about the arts and sciences? About business or sports? About education, economics, or (this was the big one) *politics*?

But the question rarely came up in the Christian circles I had been part of, and as far as I could tell, the tacit answer I got was that Christianity didn't have much to do with the secular world. People seemed to think Christianity was their side hustle.

Something about that answer never sat right with me. I knew God created the universe through Jesus and ruled it through Jesus. In practice, though, all I could conceive of Jesus ruling was my personal morality and church attendance. (By the by, he did this, in my imagination, with a bit of a scowl.) I went all the way through seminary with this question unanswered. And then I moved to Russia.

In the fall of 1998 I moved to the city of Kazan, Russia. I'll forgive you if you need to look up Kazan on your map. It's not exactly a tourist destination. But what Kazan lacked in tourist appeal it more than made up for in cultural interest. Kazan was a fascinating cultural crossroads populated by Muslims, atheists, and Orthodox Christians. Each of those communities brought their "gods" to public debates. And with a foreigner in their midst, they wanted to have debates quite often. (Just about everyone wanted to convert me.) I had been thrown into a pressure cooker of competing ideologies, which forced me to examine my own afresh.

The cultural context, however, wasn't the only factor at play. Just as influential was Kazan's, shall we say, *memorable* weather. I've heard it said that there are only three seasons in Kazan—almost winter, winter, and still winter. That's a bit of an exaggeration but only just. In the coldest part of Kazan's winters, the temperature got as low as -40. (Celsius or Fahrenheit, you ask? At 40 below, it's actually both. Behold: My storehouse of useless knowledge is voluminous.) Anyway, when winter is *that* cold and lasts *that* long, there's not much else to do but stay inside, sip Russian tea, and read.

I soon discovered some Christian thinkers that helped me build a Christian view of culture. Chief among them was the Dutch intellectual Abraham Kuyper (1837–1920). Kuyper started out as a pastor and scholar but eventually also founded and edited a national newspaper, started a private university, served as a member of Parliament, then as prime minister of the Netherlands.

Yes, he did *all* of those things. Who can compete with a career like that? But I didn't just find Kuyper's life inspiring; I found his framework of thought compelling. More than anyone else, Kuyper showed me that Christianity and culture *have* to intersect.

Kuyper emphasized that God created the universe through Jesus and that Jesus exists as King over every dimension of created life. Kuyper called those various dimensions—art, science, politics, economics, family, church, etc.—"spheres" of culture, arguing that each sphere contributes something unique and significant to human life. Jesus is Lord over each of the spheres, but he rules over each in its own unique way.

You're familiar with the book of Genesis. Think back to the first chapter, which says God created plants and animals "according to their kinds." Each species of plant or animal possesses an inner integrity and exhibits the characteristics God intended. Taken together, the world's countless varieties of life form a splendid unity in diversity, each fulfilling a particular role in the universe, each contributing to a greater whole.

Now imagine that instead of talking about plants and animals we're talking about dimensions of culture. God created them "according to their kinds" also. The Bible doesn't use that kind of terminology for culture, but it sure seems that God's pattern of ordered diversity holds true in cultural matters just as it does in botanical and zoological ones.

In Kuyper's view each sphere has its own center (distinct reason for its existence) and circumference (a limit to it's a jurisdiction). The "center" of art is to display aesthetic excellence. Science is to advance knowledge. Economics exists to steward resources, while politics exists to achieve justice. The church exists to proclaim the gospel and nurture God's people in their relationship with him. And so forth. But the "circumference" is just as critical. The church is not called to rule over the government, the arts, or the sciences. Similarly, the government is not called to rule over the church, the arts, or the sciences. And so forth. In effect, God's built a system of "checks and balances" into the world, so that no single sphere gets to have totalitarian authority over all of human life.

As I read about Kuyper's cultural spheres in that vicious Kazan winter, something clicked. I realized that Jesus, the Lord *of all*, really intended to be Lord *over all*. I had never overtly denied that truth, of course, but until Kuyper I didn't have a way to articulate how it might work in the secular world. Kuyper gave me a framework to recognize Jesus' lordship over all of life while preventing that lordship from becoming two-dimensional. He offered me a contrast from the contemporary (relativistic) American way of thinking, in which every sphere of culture seems to operate without much *center* at all. He also offered a contrast from my Russian context, where I got to see what happens when one sphere—the political one—exceeds its *circumference*.

I could say a lot more about Kuyper. It's no secret that I think he's grand. But I'll leave you to dig deeper into his thought if you want. For now, since I'm on the topic, let me wrap up by giving you three takeaways for participating in the cultural spheres.

First, you're going to find yourself interacting in multiple spheres of culture, and the way you interact differs according to the sphere. You are a member of a church, a consumer (or producer) within the economic system, a citizen of the United States, a child within a family, etc. The way you act *faithfully* may differ depending on the context. For instance, you should always love others. But the love you owe your father (family sphere) differs markedly from the love you "owe" a man who is trying to sell you something (economic sphere). Recognize that every person you interact with exists in this web of interrelated roles and that often the goals of these roles will conflict. It can get messy.

Second, when you approach the cultural spheres, you need to remember the big picture of the Bible that I mentioned a few letters back—*creation, fall, redemption, consummation*. That story line reveals basic truths about the world that apply to every sphere of culture. So when you approach a given sphere, you do so with the knowledge that (1) God made it, (2) we've broken it, and (3) God intends to redeem it and (4) will consummate its redemption when Christ returns. I find it helpful to think of those ideas in the form of questions. (1) What is God's creational design for this particular sphere? (2) How have God's designs been misdirected and corrupted by our sin? (3) In what ways can we redirect this sphere toward Christ's intentions for it? Answering the questions is never simple, but it provides a useful place to start.

Third, you have two resources at your disposal when engaging culture. Theologians call them general revelation and special revelation. The latter is the revealed truth of the Bible. While universally true, it is not exhaustively so. C. S. Lewis put it well, saying, "When [Christianity] tells you to feed the hungry, it doesn't give you lessons in cookery. If you want to learn *that*, you must go to a cook."[1] Cookery, as Lewis calls it, falls under the heading of general revelation. We learn certain truths better by investigating God's world. It's wise for us to ask what economic systems have turned oppressive in the past, what science teaches us about the way our bodies work, or what business models are likely to do to family life. So use the Bible and apply it to every sphere of culture. But be prepared to do the tough work of investigating God's world, too.

I think that's enough for now. I'm hoping you don't have to travel as far as Kazan to come to the same realization I did. Though if you're headed that way, let me know. I wouldn't mind an excuse to go back there for a spell. It may have been cold, but I loved the place.

I look forward to hearing from you soon.

Yours,

Bruce

CHAPTER 5

THE ONE POLITICAL RALLY AMERICAN CHRISTIANS SHOULDN'T SKIP

Christian,

I apologize that I haven't been able to respond sooner. If you'll believe it, there are actually times when we professors have to log some hours and do an honest day's work. You know how grueling it is to crank out a fifteen-page paper the night before it's due? Well, imagine having to *read* that same paper, and seventy-five similar papers, while offering constructive feedback on each page. Many of these papers are terrific, but others bear the marks of having been written in an overcaffeinated delirium at 3:00 a.m. I have a theory that if forced to grade enough papers in succession, a professor may literally die from tedium. It's like being stoned to death with Ping-Pong balls.

Anyway, I'm glad you enjoyed my little autobiographical diversion. My heart was strangely warmed thinking of the cold nights I spent in Kazan, finally seeing the connection between religion and politics in a fresh way.

Now for *your* letter. I really enjoyed the details of the "religion and politics" debate you had with Professor Baileywick in the political science department. Baileywick is a bigwig in that community, if you didn't already know. He's written more books than most people have *read*. So I understand your being a bit intimidated. But when he began to describe your views as "scary stuff"—that, Christian, should raise the question of how good of an education is being offered at Dupont. Is it a genuine liberal-arts education or merely indoctrination from one point of view? In fact, if you'll remember, a few years ago a national news outlet revealed that Dupont's political science faculty is composed of forty-three Democrats and—[drum roll]—*one* Republican. That's a little odd, eh? No wonder your professor thinks your views are so exotic and so scary. He's teaching in an echo chamber!

Fortunately, the political science department is not your most important political community. That honor is reserved for your local church. That's right. I said it. The local church is the most important political community in our nation.

Now, I *don't* mean to say that local churches should fancy themselves public policy centers or political think tanks; churches are neither called nor competent for those purposes. Remember what we learned from Kuyper about the various spheres? Churches who attempt such things lose their character as the church and produce sloppy policy to boot. It's a lose-lose.

What I *do* mean to say is that local churches are political at a deeper and more profound level than political parties, think tanks, or election cycles. The church is political in the sense that it is the only divinely instituted embassy for Christ's kingship. And for that reason it is the one politi-cal assembly in which every Christian American should participate.

You probably haven't ever heard the church referred to as a "political assembly." But remember the political nature of Jesus' life and ministry. He lived and ministered in the con-text of the world's greatest superpower, the Roman Empire. So when Jesus preached "the good news of the kingdom" (Matt. 4:23) and declared that God's kingdom was at hand (Matt. 3:2), everybody understood that he was announcing a political kingdom of some sort. Not a single person listening to him envisioned an apolitical series of revival meetings. N. T. Wright writes:

> Jesus' message was after all inescapably political. He denounced rulers, real and self-appointed. He spoke of good news for the poor. He led large groups of people off into the wilderness, a sure sign of revolu-tionary intent. He announced the imminent destruc-tion of the Jerusalem temple. At the start of a festival celebrating Israel's liberation, he organized around himself what could only have looked like a royal pro-cession. And he deliberately and dramatically acted out a parable of the temple's destruction, thus draw-ing on to himself the anger of the authorities in a way which he could never have done by healing lepers and forgiving prostitutes (though we should not miss the revolutionary note in his offer of forgiveness, whose real offence lay in its bypassing of the temple cult). . . . He died the death of the *lestai*, the political insurrec-tionists (Barabbas, and the two crucified with Jesus, were *lestai*). How could he not have been "political"?[1]

Even though Jesus did not run for political office, build an army, or lead a public advocacy group (thank God), his ministry was political in the deepest and most profound sense of the word: it was designed to reveal that Jesus himself is the true King of the whole world. His political authority relativizes every other political claim.

It's why Paul told the Philippian Christians (Philippi was a Roman colony) that the day will come when every person will confess that Jesus—rather than Caesar—is Lord (Phil. 2:10–11). In fact, the early church grasped Jesus' political claims to such an extent that Paul had to remind them to give proper respect to the Roman government and resist the temptation toward anarchy (Rom. 13:1).

If that were true of Jesus—the founder of our faith—and true of his first followers, doesn't it make sense that God's set-apart community today, the local church, would be similarly political?

Now your political science professors are going to think this is *really* "scary stuff." They'll think it is scary because they are educated in the school of secular modernity, which, for all its gestures toward tolerance, is a totalizing worldview that will brook no compromise with Christianity. Even though Christianity gave birth to the modern West, the child has grown up to abuse its parents. But enough about your professors' worldviews. More on that later.

The deeply political nature of Jesus' ministry suggests that his community—the church—would also be, in some sense, political. The question is, *In what sense?* In order to answer that question, Christian, it's helpful to view the church as both an organization and an organism. The two elements of the local church will function politically in quite different ways.

When we attend church for the Sunday morning gathering, we are experiencing the church as an *organization*. This organization nourishes our primary political identity—ambassadors of Christ the King—and does so in very specific ways outlined by the Bible.

When we attend church, we come face-to-face with other citizens of God's kingdom, learning to love them and respect them despite our social, cultural, ethnic, and economic differences. We listen to a sermon in which the pastor (ideally, at least) reminds us that the Bible provides the true story of the whole world, a story in which Christ is at the center. We take the Lord's Supper, in which we are reminded that the King shed his blood on our behalf and will return one day to reconstitute the world under a reign of peace and justice. We adjourn with prayer, understanding that we are being sent out into the world as emissaries of the King.

So the church as an organization is "political" in a profound but limited manner. Its political nature is profound because it is an embassy of Christ's kingdom, reminding us and encouraging us to find our identity in him. Its political nature is limited, though, because local churches are not designed (or competent) to rule the nation, translate the Bible's moral teaching into public policy, or defend the nation from enemy attack. Those tasks fall out of the church's organizational jurisdiction. To borrow from Kuyper's language, it is both beyond the church's *circumference* as well as untrue to the church's *center* to dictate public policy.

Yet the church's political influence doesn't end there. The church is not only an organization but also an *organism*. Another way to put this is to think of the church *gathered* and the church *scattered*. Both are the church, but they act differently. When members of a church adjourn, we are sent out into the world as ambassadors of the King.

The exact nature of our ambassadorship will differ from church member to church member; it depends on our competency and circumstances. For most church members our ambassadorship can be summed up as "being good Christian citizens." Our primary allegiance to Christ motivates us and guides us in our coffee-shop conversations, Facebook interactions, political-party involvement, and voting decisions. Our love for him and our loyalty to his Word shape our family life, work ethic, leisure and entertainment, reading habits, and neighborhood involvement. Our embrace of the gospel causes us to serve fellow citizens who are financially disadvantaged or socially marginalized; it spurs us to share the Christian gospel with others. Each of us can—and should—perform these sorts of political actions.

Other church members, however, can serve our nation in more specifically political ways. Some members are directly involved in politics, serving as politicians, political staffers, policy wonks, judges, or lawyers. Others serve in related fields such as political journalism. These members are uniquely positioned to serve our nation politically. Their primary allegiance to Christ should motivate and guide the way they craft public policy, engage in public debate, and interact with their constituency.

In other words, Sunday morning public worship prepares us for Monday morning public life. Sunday morning worship reminds us that the Bible is the true story of the whole world and that Jesus stands at the center of that story as the King of the world. Monday morning public life provides the opportunity for Christians to allow the Bible's story and Jesus' kingship to shape the way we speak and act in the public square. After gathering to bask in Christ's light together, we are prepared to disperse for the rest of the week to reflect the "light of the world" together in our respective stations of life.

I doubt Professor Baileywick agrees with this assessment. But if he could open his mind just a little bit, maybe he could see that this way of thinking is not "scary stuff." This way of thinking should, in fact, prevent some of the ham-fisted and misguided ways Christians in the past have attempted to influence politics. History, of course, provides plenty of examples of both Christians and non-Christians who have wreaked havoc in the political realm. Baileywick is afraid you'll re-create the Spanish Inquisition. Fair enough. But we must also protect against the terrors of anti-Christian political ideologies like those of the Nazis, Josef Stalin, and Pol Pot—just to name a few. The point is this: a citizen or politician who is genuinely committed to the biblical Jesus will have unique motivation and special resources to serve our nation well.

Well, I'll wrap it up for now. You mentioned that you're in the midst of writing research papers. Do me a favor, would you? Since you've got a "target" on you now (you're a—gasp!—*evangelical* Christian), do your best to turn in excellent papers. Make sure your research is first-rate. Choose an interesting topic and make sure your writing is lucid and engaging, OK? If you don't, your prof will go to sleep faster than a ferret swimming in a bucket of Thorazine. More importantly, he won't respect you.

Yours,

Bruce

PS: You mentioned the "separation of church and state" in your last letter. Now *that's* a rich phrase with an intriguing history. I could ramble on about it for a while, so let me know if you want my take.

CHAPTER 6

SWIM IN YOUR OWN LANE, PLEASE

Christian,

Well, you bit. You just couldn't resist hearing what gems of wisdom I had to offer on the relationship of church and state. Just remember: You asked for it.

Your question about church and state was a keen one. You are right: questions about church and state are not the same as questions about religion and politics, although the public debate often collapses the two together. Even though politics cannot be separated from religion, the state *should* be kept separate from the church (and vice versa).

That's a simple enough plan for fair play, right? Well, as one of our generation's prophets, Mike Tyson, put it, "Everyone has a plan till they get punched in the mouth." Keeping church and state separate may seem simple, but living it out gets messy in a hurry.

But before we get more into the specifics, let me say that I had a good laugh from your description of the radio talk shows you've been following. Your description of the various hosts—"he is cruelly depriving a village somewhere of an idiot" and "she asks such deep questions but gives such incandescently shallow answers"—were very colorful if not a little bit overstated.

You're right that everyone is entitled to be a chump from time to time, but some people really abuse the privilege. To their credit, however, they're only giving the American people what we're asking for. They are, in a sense, the monsters we have created. These pundits provide politically polarized sound bites that confirm their audience's prejudices. The audience "wins" because their opinions are confirmed rather than challenged. The talk shows win because they continue to draw large audiences and, therefore, maintain their advertising revenue. In the end, however, American democracy loses.

And this phenomenon of polarized and superficial rhetoric is nowhere more prevalent than in discussions of church and state. On the one hand, many Americans seem to want the Christian church to take the reins of power, turning the gospel pulpit into a platform for political activism and public policy pronouncements. On the other hand, just as many citizens seem to want the church to go away, to be excluded from the zoning ordinances, literally and figuratively.

What should a Christian American make of this issue? Well, let's start by taking a quick look at the United States Constitution; then we'll turn to the Bible to see how it applies.

The United States Constitution and its Amendments address "religion" in several passages, and these passages are the basis for conversations about "church and state":

- "[N]o religious Test shall ever be required as a Qualification to any Office or public Trust under the United States." (Article VI, Clause 3)

- "Congress shall make no law respecting an establishment of religion, or prohibiting the free exercise
thereof; or abridging the freedom of speech . . . ;
or the right of the people peaceably to assemble."
(Amendment I)

The first passage—which, by the way, contains the only
reference to religion in the original Constitution—makes clear
that the federal government should not impose a religious
test for public officeholders. In effect, this means we cannot
require officeholders to be Christians, seculars, Catholics, or
Protestants; neither can we *restrict* officeholders who hold
those commitments. These are important parameters, but
the scope here is admittedly small. The second passage is
drawn from the First Amendment to the Constitution. Some
Americans talk about the framers of the Constitution as if
they thought religion was bad for the public square. As if
they didn't have the consensus to abolish religion but, given
the chance, would have been happy to do it. This interpretation is simply wrong. A close reading of history and of the
Constitution leads us to understand that many of the framers were trying to keep us from becoming a European-style
government in which a particular Christian denomination is
established by the federal government.

So the framers were not trying to abolish religion from
the public square. Consider George Washington's first
inaugural address (1789), which he dedicated to the "Great
Author of every public and private good," and his Farewell
Address (1796), in which he declared, "Of all the disposi-
tions and habits which lead to political prosperity, Religion
and morality are indispensable supports." These comments
exemplified how most of his contemporaries—including most
of the founders—viewed religion's place in public life. And

there is nothing in the First Amendment's legislative history that puts it at odds with Washington's view.

Granted, some Americans employ the phrase "separation of church and state" to argue that religion should be pushed out of the public square, that government should not support faith-based charities or educational initiatives, and so on. But the Constitution does not call for this sort of strict separation.

Only recently has any legal body considered this kind of strict separation even possible. In *Everson v. Board of Education* (1947), the Supreme Court began to interpret the First Amendment "establishment" clause in terms of a "separation of church and state." The Court relied on a single phrase found in a solitary letter written by one lonely founder, Thomas Jefferson, to the Danbury Baptist Association of Connecticut (1802). In the letter Jefferson wrote about a "wall of separation between church and state." If you ask me, that's a pretty flimsy foundation when compared to, well, *the actual Constitution.*

As Christians, though, we aren't duty bound to agree with the Constitution in every respect. It's not an inerrant document. We should, on the other hand, ask what the Bible has to say about the relationship of "religion and politics" and "church and state." I'll tackle those phrases one at a time.

As for *religion and politics*, the Bible does not lead us toward a *strict* separation. It does not support the view that citizens should lay aside their religious beliefs in the public square or that government should never support faith-based initiatives. In fact, it says the opposite. As I mentioned in one of my previous letters, all people are incurably religious in one way or another, and all people's religion radiates outward into their public life. So we couldn't posit a strict separation even if we wanted to. We might as well try to

maintain a separation of "language and politics." It's a logi-
cal absurdity. Plus, as Christians, we know our faith should
function as a deep well of motivation and guidance as we
seek the common good of our nation.

Now, when it comes to *church and state*, the Bible speaks
to the matter indirectly, suggesting a healthy separation
of the two. Remember Abraham Kuyper's approach to the
various spheres of culture, which I wrote about amid my
sentimental reflections on Kazan? Kuyper believed that God
created each sphere of culture with its own center (unique
reason for being) and circumference (limit to its jurisdiction). Like any other sphere of culture, church and state have
their own unique reasons for being and their own unique
jurisdictions.

I think Kuyper is right. God has given churches and governments unique reasons for being and unique jurisdictions
that correspond with those reasons. Church and government
should swim in their own lanes!

The relevance of this separation can hardly be overstated.
On the one hand, ecclesiastical leaders and churches are not
called by God to make public-policy decisions or defend the
nation against attack. They should not try to take the place of
the government or control it. God doesn't desire it, and they
simply aren't much good at it. On the other hand, governments and political leaders are not called by God to appoint
pastors, baptize church members, or interpret the Bible. They
should not seek to take the place of the church or control it.
God doesn't desire it, and they simply aren't much good at it.

Now this type of separation might seem intuitive and
obvious for you. Congratulations, you have proved your
American credentials. But I assure you this hasn't always
been the automatic understanding of church and state. More
importantly, many of our fellow citizens today do not see

things this way. So let's circle back to each of the main errors, which I will call "statism" and "ecclesiasticism."

Statism is a situation in which the government or "state" goes beyond its jurisdiction by interfering with the other spheres of human activity. In fact, without Constitutional restrictions and left to its own devices, government tends to inflate its own importance and interfere with areas that are not its concern. Like a giant octopus, its tentacles begin to reach into every nook and cranny of human existence. Governments seem invariably tilted toward acquiring more power for themselves.

Most of the time, that is. In some instances the government is not only *allowed* but is *obligated* to interfere in the other spheres, at least in a limited manner. Kuyper enumerated a few of these instances.

First, he argued, the government may adjudicate disputes between the spheres. For example, it might step in to settle a dispute between the spheres of business and family by restricting a bar (business) from playing loud music past a certain hour in the evening (for the sake of the family). Similarly, it might resolve a dispute between the spheres of business and education by refusing a permit to an adult video store (business) that wishes to operate near an elementary school (education).

Second, he argued that the government may adjudicate disputes within a sphere. Usually, this type of adjudication involves protecting the weak from the strong. The government, for instance, might intervene in a family's life in order to keep a parent from abusing a child. Similarly, it might make regulations that restrict adolescents from working in certain types of dangerous business environments.

Third, the government might adjudicate issues that don't fit well within any one sphere or that involve more than one cultural sphere. For example, the government is justified in taxing citizens in order to build roads and bridges that will profit every sphere.

But beyond these limited circumstances, the government should respect its limited jurisdiction, especially in relation to churches. It has no business deciding who can or cannot become a church member, who can or cannot be a pastor, and what is or is not the right way to interpret the Bible's teaching on a moral issue. That government officials have the *desire* to do these things doesn't give them any more authority to do so than my childhood desire to play for the nineties-era Chicago Bulls guaranteed me a spot next to Michael Jordan.

Ecclesiasticism is a mirror image of statism. Whereas statism is a situation in which the government exceeds its proper limits, ecclesiasticism is a circumstance in which the church oversteps its bounds. Think about the Middle Ages: in many medieval kingdoms, the institutional church involved itself in political power plays and public-policy decisions. In some instances it even had the power to dictate public policy to the state.

There are at least four problems with ecclesiasticism: first, the church is not called by God to govern the nations; no biblical teaching supports ecclesiastical rulership of a nation-state.

Second, it is not competent to govern the nation. It is competent to teach biblical truths (and this only by the power of the Spirit), but it is not generally competent to determine how those truths should be applied in a twenty-first-century constitutional democratic republic.

Third, ecclesiastical states tend to become tyrannical; they make laws that require non-Christians to live as if they were believers.

Fourth, ecclesiasticism creates a situation that encourages false professions of faith. Because of the church's domination of the public square, nonbelievers are tempted to identify as Christians in order to get the "social perks" of their newly acquired religious identity.

But the church gets a bit of an exception, just like the government does. The church transcends the other spheres, including the political sphere, in one critical way. If you recall, the church is both an organization and an organism. As an organization that has its own leadership and meets weekly with its members, the church should remain separate from the state. But as an organism whose members scatter throughout the various spheres of culture during the week, the church has an indirect but significant influence on all of those spheres, including the political sphere. You simply can't keep the church confined to four walls. It wasn't possible in the first century, and it isn't possible now.

So, Christian, all of that is to say: Christians should affirm that the government and the church should each respect its own center and circumference. More often than not both tend to overreach and need to step back and settle down. They've got enough on their plates without trying to borrow from each other.

I think I need to wrap up this letter. I realize I didn't answer the other questions you asked, most of which involved how your Christianity should inform your views on some of the "hot button" political issues and policy debates of our day. But you probably already know that we can't do any of them justice unless we take them each in turn. The good news is I'm happy to tackle them one at a time. But first, I'm going to settle in to watch some March Madness.

I know you've got another research paper due this week. So, why don't we pick the conversation back up after you've finished? If you don't hear from me in about a week, you have my permission to send a carrier pigeon in pursuit.

Yours,

Bruce

CHAPTER 7

LET GOD BE TRUE AND
EVERY IDEOLOGY A LIAR

Christian,

With the research paper in your rearview mirror, I imagine you are exhausted from late-night research sessions but also energized to tackle the rest of the semester. The verve and wit of your letter, however, make me think you're more energized than exhausted. That's good.

You're right. A lot of younger Americans are drawn toward socialism. They have good intentions, but I'm afraid they don't understand the long-term negative consequences of adopting a socialist model. I've heard it said that a socialist is a person who is so outraged by the way money and power are controlled by a few corporations that he proposes to place nearly all of the money and power into the hands of one giant corporation—the federal government.

So, you're right that socialism is problematic. But I think you need to be an equal opportunity offender here. Let's critique socialism, but let's also critique America's other dominant ideologies.

Years ago, I picked up a book titled *Political Visions and Illusions*, written by a Christian political scientist, David Koyzis. Once I picked it up, I couldn't put it down. In it, Koyzis subjected each of our era's dominant political ideologies to a thorough "idol-critique."

You and I have talked about idols and idolatry before, Christian. But by way of reminder, when the Bible talks about idolatry, it is referring to the way humans tend to ascribe ultimacy to some aspect of God's creation instead of ascribing it to God alone. In other words, rather than worshipping God as God, we pick some good created thing—sex, money, power—and we "idolize it," allowing it to command our loyalties and shape our lives.

Koyzis's fine point is that political ideologies are a lot like individuals. They tend to ascribe ultimacy to some aspect of God's world. Once they have ascribed ultimacy to their chosen idol, they look to it to "save" our society by eradicating "evils" that threaten their idol. And "We the People" are tempted to embrace these ideologies as political saviors.

Four of the most prevalent political ideologies in the United States today are liberalism, conservatism, nationalism, and socialism. These ideologies aren't created equal, but they share this in common: they are good servants but bad masters.

Let's start with classical political liberalism; after all, other prominent political ideologies either developed from within it or arose directly as a reaction against it. In its earlier forms liberalism arose from within the Christian tradition and was not idolatrous. By definition it denoted commitment to a constitutional and representative government that emphasized liberty and personal freedom. Yet liberalism quickly took on ideological dimensions by absolutizing an individual's independence—his or her "right" to be free from external control or influence.

One problem with liberalism is its overemphasis on the individual. This overemphasis reduces society to little more than a collection of autonomous individuals and government to a "necessary evil." You see, early on liberals insisted that government should be minimal, existing only to protect individuals and their property. This logically flows from the foundation; if the greatest good is an individual's freedom, government should be as small as possible so as not to interfere.

Ironically, however, liberals soon began expanding the size of government to protect individuals from more ambiguous threats, such as lack of resources. Eventually liberals came to expect the government to accommodate their personal desires and to do so in a religiously and morally neutral manner. Thus, when a person's poor judgment or immoral choices cause negative consequences, liberals expect the government to ameliorate or even eliminate the consequences. ("Have you fathered five children out of wedlock? Not a problem. The government is happy to tax other citizens to help ease the consequences, but it's even happier to take those children's lives in the womb beforehand.")

Ideological liberalism, therefore, has proved to be self-defeating. It began by exalting individual autonomy but ironically ended up expanding the role of the government continually in order to mitigate the increasingly negative consequences stemming from individuals' unwise or immoral choices.

This type of progressive liberalism, which bears little resemblance to liberalism in its initial and nonideological form, functions as a false system of salvation. It craves absolute independence from social norms, identifies social norms and authorities as the "root evil" of society, and places its trust in ideologically liberal political parties that promise to maximize free choice.

In its worst forms contemporary liberalism wants to get rid of God and religion so that individuals can freely "create" themselves (for example, they celebrate as heroes those persons who attempt to change their biological gender). As a result citizens in a politically liberal regime lose freedom as government inevitably swells to enormous proportions, and they experience a degraded civic life because of the combination of hyperindividualism, vanishing community, swelling government, and disintegrating moral norms.

I hope you're still with me because now I'm going to start stepping on some toes. Let's talk about conservatism. Conservatism is often viewed as the polar opposite of liberalism. Yet, as Koyzis notes, conservatism is not a single, stable, or unified ideology we can encapsulate in an identifiable doctrinal position. It doesn't even qualify strictly as an ideology because it operates as a sort of tendency that feeds off other ideologies.

Its tendency is to "conserve" the social norms and cultural heritage of a particular nation, and usually it seeks to conserve a particular era of that nation's heritage. In other words, pure ideological "conservatism" tends to deify a certain era in national life, ascribe evil to any type of grand social-reform agendas, and place its trust in ideologically conservative political parties that promise to undercut social reform agendas and protect the nation's cultural heritage.

One problem with pure conservatism is that it is always on the move. It is less an abstract ideology and more a contextual response. In fact, what counts as conservatism in one country will have little to do with conservatism in another country. While conservatives in the United States might be trying to conserve the economic and political policies of the Reagan era, conservatives in another country might be trying to revitalize the Stalinism of an earlier era, conserving, as it were, authoritarian socialist communism. What a society aims to conserve will vary wildly depending on the nation and its history.

But, to get to the point, let's consider American conservatism. As you know, the views I express in our letter exchanges fall on the conservative side of the American political spectrum. We conservatives are having the most difficult time making tactical—much less strategic—alliance with one another. One group of conservatives wants to conserve classical liberalism and its emphasis on individual freedom. Another group wants to conserve certain moral norms. Others want to conserve white identity in our increasingly diverse society. Still others want to conserve the small-government agenda of the Reagan administration.

The problem with pure ideological conservatism is that on its own it lacks transcendent principles. In spite of conservatives' high view of the past, they know intuitively that they cannot uncritically accept all of it. So when they do criticize some aspect of the past (e.g., slavery), they are forced to rummage around for some transcendent norms. That's why pure conservatives have often found themselves in tactical alliance with Christians, drawing upon Christianity's transcendent norms when and where they pair well with their agenda. Regardless, a pure social conservatism elevates cultural heritage to a level of ultimacy reserved for God alone, and for that reason it has a twisting and distorting effect socially and culturally.

As you and I exchange letters, I am trying to show you what it might look like to employ your Christian way of thinking to ensure that your conservative approach to politics is healthy rather than idolatrous. More on that later.

What about nationalism? It is experiencing quite a resurgence in recent years in some conservative quarters. Nationalism is an ideology that emphasizes a "nation" and usually identifies one criterion—such as language, culture, race, homeland, constitutional order—as the unifying feature of the nation. Nationalism becomes idolatrous when people begin to worship the nation, in effect viewing it as the savior that will protect them from being corrupted or influenced by people who are different from them.

In America, nationalism sometimes manifests itself as an excessive allegiance to the United States as a nation or idea. This variety of nationalists usually views their nation as superior to other nations in the ability to exemplify some transcendent value. Usually, this value is freedom. Because our nation possesses the highest virtue, the argument goes, our nation must therefore be God's favorite. This sort of thinking goes beyond patriotism (which is healthy and good) by glorifying the nation.

Other times, nationalism manifests itself as a disproportionate allegiance to an ethnic group. Think about the reemergence of white nationalism in the past decade and especially during the 2016 election cycle. Proponents such as Jared Taylor and Richard Spencer argue that black communities are uncivilized and have corrupted our nation and, therefore, white people should resist the degrading influence of black culture by giving preference to whites and white culture.

This type of ethno-nationalism functions as a false religion. It seeks justice, which is noble and reasonable, but it doesn't value or protect those who are not of its own kind. A Christian view of politics resists nationalist idolatry by refusing to deify the nation or locate its root evil in "other-ness," by rejecting political platforms or politicians who aspire to restore the nation's greatness by giving preference to one group of citizens over another. A proper Christian patriotism will engender a humble love of one's nation rather than arrogant or unjust forms of nationalism.

Finally, socialism. Just as the American Right is experiencing a surging nationalism within its ranks, the American Left is experiencing an upswell of socialism.

Socialism comes in many varieties. Some versions take a revolutionary approach while others take a more gradual and peaceful approach to undermining the free market. Some base their claims in science while others base their claims in philosophy or religion. Nonetheless, all variations of socialism have one thing in common: a political agenda that centers on redistributing society's wealth in order to force economic equality among its citizens.

Karl Marx, the patriarch of socialism, was relentlessly critical of the free market, which he called "capitalism." You're aware, of course, that Marx accused the free market of dehumanizing human beings by alienating them from their labor. In his view proponents of a free market value money and wealth acquisition more than we value our workers. As he saw it, businessmen tend to treat workers as mere business expenses rather than as human beings, as faceless machines to be manipulated, replaced, or eliminated.

You might not be aware that Marx also notes that capitalism *undermines national identities and cultural distinctives* by encouraging people to clamor for wealth rather than honoring national identity and cultural distinctives. Given his comments about national identity and cultural distinctives, it is interesting to note that socialist regimes (such as the former Soviet Union) have tended to glorify the state.

To get to the point: socialism makes a god out of material equality and considers economic inequality the greatest evil. It then points to "wealth redistribution by taxation" or "communal ownership" as the saviors who can rescue society from its ills.

The problem is that wealth redistribution and communal ownership don't happen by themselves. No, they must be forced upon society by the government. Read the history books, Christian. Marxist socialism is totalizing—employing coercive power in its micromanagement of every dimension of human life—and radical—wanting to reconstruct society from the roots up. Ironically, after having reconstructed society by redistributing wealth, it actually harms the economies of the nations that adopt it as an official ideology; although socialism increased "equality" in those nations, it was the type of equality that ships experience when they all *sink* with a receding tide.

Now, don't get me wrong. I'm not saying all of our modern political ideologies are thoroughly wrong and bad. No, each ideology has good intentions and good insights, but at the same time those intentions and insights are corrupted by the ideologies' inevitable tendency to elevate one idea to the level of a god and then use that god to beat back anything that restricts it.

So what's a politically interested Christian like you or me supposed to do? Well, what I'm trying to do in our letter exchanges is to help you approach American politics and public life in a way that resists idolizing any one good, whether that be individual freedom, cultural heritage, material prosperity, or national and ethnic identity. I'm trying to help you construct a political paradigm that recognizes God's sovereignty over our nation, draws on our Christianity to work for the common good, and respects the dignity and rights of citizens who have differing visions of the common good.

I'm insufficient for the task. I'm just one Christian, one public theologian, trying to think through the issues. For this task we will need to raise up a generation of Christian political theorists and public theologians who view the gospel as a public truth that challenges the whole of society rather than a private truth that speaks only to our inner experience.

We need Christian thinkers who will soak themselves in the biblical narrative and Christian tradition so that they will be able, reflexively and intuitively, to challenge the reigning narratives of the politicians, parties, and cable news networks. So they will counteract the foolishness that dominates our nation's public square and the incivility that degrades our public discourse.

Koyzis did a masterful job of this in *Political Visions and Illusions*. You really should get a copy. I'm hoping we see a generation of political theorists and politically informed Christians follow his lead, and the lead of others like him, in carving out a better political path for the future than the paths we are currently offered.

Yours,

Bruce

PART 2

A CHRISTIAN VIEW ON
HOT-BUTTON ISSUES

CHAPTER 8

IF YOU CAN KEEP IT

Christian,

It's been a while since we last communicated. Sounds like you've been busy. Speaking of which, congratulations on completing your final exams! I'm happy for you, and I only wish you'd taken a few days' vacation before beginning your internship at Conservative Cable News Network (CCNN).

More than anything, I am happy that you've finally found a church home—The Pinnacle Church—that is close enough to the university for you to be involved on a regular basis. I notice that despite its denominationally generic name, it's a Baptist church. That is a nice coincidence, given the fact that you asked if I'd put "religious liberty" at the top of the list for our summer discussion of fifteen hot-button political issues.

Why is this such a nice coincidence, you ask? I'm sure you won't learn this at Dupont (perish the thought), but Baptists actually led the way in promoting religious liberty in our nation. In 1644, for example, Baptist pastor Roger Williams argued that God commands Christians to grant freedom of religion to everybody, including not only Christians but "paganish, Jewish, Turkish [i.e., Muslim], or anti-christian consciences." A century later another Baptist pastor, John

Leland, led a movement to end the federal government's persecution of religious dissenters through the First Amendment to the U.S. Constitution.

This shouldn't be surprising for anybody who knows church history, although that's a rather small circle, especially at Dear Old Dupont. During the sixteenth century in Europe, one of *your* Baptist forebears, Balthasar Hübmaier, argued that religious liberty should be secured for all types of Christians and even for Muslims. If Christians wish to change a person's mind, Hübmaier argued, we should do so via persuasion rather than coercion.[1]

Why do Baptists and other Christians believe in religious liberty? You can probably guess based on some of the letters I've already written. For one thing we believe God created different spheres of culture, each of which has limits to its jurisdiction. Unless there are exceptional situations, the government shouldn't be messing with the religious sphere. It's out of bounds.

For another thing, as Christians we recognize that the gospel is freely given and freely received. A truly Christian citizenry would not *want* its government to force other citizens to "embrace" the Christian gospel; a true embrace can only be offered and received freely. Forced love, when we encounter it in the natural world, is rightly labeled "rape." Why would we assume that forcing spiritual love is somehow different?

Fortunately, Christian, the United States Constitution was tailor-made to protect religious liberty. The First Amendment to the United States Constitution declares, "Congress shall make no law respecting an establishment of religion, or prohibiting the free exercise thereof." Take note: the amendment defines religious liberty as the free *exercise* of religion. It does not restrict religious freedom by confining it to privately held beliefs or semipublic worship services. The Constitution is clear. Religious freedom extends to public actions.

Religious liberty is a "first freedom" because it stands at the center of what it means to be human. As a constitutional freedom, it declares each person has value and dignity, each person is free to hold his or her own convictions about ultimate reality, and each person is guaranteed the liberty to align his or her life with those convictions. And just as importantly, each of us is free to do so openly, without fear.

When religious freedom is threatened, every other freedom is threatened as well. More than any other sphere of life, religion has the power to check the government's perpetual intrusion on the liberties of individuals, groups, and mediating institutions.

That fact probably helps explain one of Benjamin Franklin's most famous statements. After the Constitutional Convention concluded and Franklin emerged from the building that day, a Mrs. Powell confronted him, asking, "Well, doctor, what have we got? A republic or a monarchy?" Franklin responded, "A republic madam—if you can keep it."

Without freedom of religion, every other freedom is threatened as well.

Which brings us to an important point. Religious liberty is, in fact, being threatened from both the Left and the Right. On the Right the most significant danger is found in arguments that our government should secure religious liberty for Christians but not for others. On the Left many people want to reinterpret the Constitution's freedom of "religious exercise" by restricting it to freedom of "worship," thereby pushing religion out of the realm of public action. But this won't work because, in one way or another, every world religion affects the private *and* public lives of its adherents. Christianity, for example, makes clear that true worship involves offering our whole selves, all of the time, to God (Rom. 12:1).

The Supreme Court has been a recent ally in restricting religious exercise. So have many of America's most powerful corporations. There's a real chance that religious liberty—not just for Christians but for all people—ends up being politically homeless, with neither major political party defending it or protecting it.

You might think it an overstatement to say that religious liberty is seriously threatened in our nation, and the Supreme Court has been among the worst offenders. I won't be surprised if you need some persuading on this point. It's not a claim you'll hear much within the "diverse" political science faculty at Dupont.

Think about the *Obergefell v. Hodges* (June 2015) case. The Court handed down a 5–4 decision in which the majority asserted that same-sex couples had a fundamental right to marriage. Of course, the majority claimed to have "found" this right in the Constitution. Yet, as we can discuss another time, they take a view of the Constitution that allows them to *reinterpret* it "in light of the times" rather than *interpreting* it in the way our founders would have at the time of its adoption. In this one decision the Supreme Court reinterpreted the Constitution and forever altered the definition and nature of marriage in America. Beyond the historical novelty of this ruling, it is problematic that such an important issue was taken up by *the Court* instead of allowing the American *people* to handle it democratically, through the legislative process as outlined by the Constitution. Does it sound like a democratic republic to you when the will of five people outweighs a majority of the nation? Remember, it's only a republic *if you can keep it.*

More to the point, Chief Justice Roberts's dissenting opinion notes that the *Obergefell* ruling had quite a bit to say about religious liberty—and not in a good way. "The majority," Roberts wrote, "suggests that religious believers may continue to 'advocate' and 'teach' their views of marriage. The First Amendment guarantees, however, the freedom to 'exercise' religion. Ominously, that is not a word the majority uses. Unfortunately, people of faith can take no comfort in the treatment they receive from the majority today."

Similarly, Justice Alito wrote, "I assume that those who cling to old beliefs will be able to whisper their thoughts in the recesses of their homes, but if they repeat those views in public, they will risk being labeled as bigots and treated as such by governments, employers, and schools. . . . [T]he Nation will experience bitter and lasting wounds."

Those are some strong words by Justices Roberts and Alito. My guess is your secular progressive friends think they're being paranoid. Your professors, too. But I think Roberts and Alito are right.

For example, the U.S. Commission on Civil Rights (USCCR) recently released a report entitled "Peaceful Coexistence: Reconciling Nondiscrimination Principles with Civil Liberties." In the report USCCR Chairman Martin R. Castro (no relation) writes, "The phrases 'religious liberty' and 'religious freedom' will stand for nothing except hypocrisy so long as they remain code words for discrimination, intolerance, racism, sexism, homophobia, Islamophobia, Christian supremacy or any form of intolerance."[2] Castro thinks it's just fine to restrict religious freedom whenever and wherever he and his secular progressive friends deem it "bigoted" or "phobic."

That raises the question: *Is religious liberty really just a mask for intolerance?* When a baker refuses to bake a cake for a gay wedding, one side claims "religious liberty" while the other cries, "Bigotry!" Who is right?

I'm sure there are some bigoted bakers out there. But a truly *evangelical* concern for religious liberty doesn't come from a place of hate. Our defense of religious freedom is motivated by our conviction that religion is a heartfelt reality, which by its very nature radiates outward into our public speech and actions. We cannot bifurcate the private from the public. We cannot in good conscience restrict the exercise of our religion to our homes and churches.

Neither should our defense of religious liberty be dismissed as some sort of special pleading. This is where many of our conservative friends aren't doing us any favors. The more they deny religious liberty to those outside of Christianity, the more it appears that the "religious liberty" we want is really just preferential treatment for *our* group. To paraphrase the apostle Paul, their mockery is deserved (cf. Rom. 3:8).

When we defend religious liberty, we do so because we know the erosion of religious liberty will have an enormous negative effect *on everyone.* If the secular progressive agenda moves forward and its restrictive view of religious liberty takes hold, religious believers will find themselves unable to exercise their religion without serious social, cultural, legal, and economic repercussions.

Consider, for example, the implications for religiously conservative institutions of higher education. These institutions have confessional statements that conflict with the reigning progressive prejudices concerning, for example, sexual behavior or abortifacient contraceptives. As the progressive view of "religious liberty" takes hold, these institutions may be stripped of their tax-exempt status, or forfeit their accreditation, if the federal government determines the doctrinal standards of such institutions are "hateful"—i.e., too far out of step with progressive orthodoxy. In addition to these issues, these institutions will likely lose revenue because of the "donor stigma" associated with giving to conservative causes.[3] These are not minor inconveniences.

But perhaps it sounds like I'm appealing for preferential treatment again. Not so fast. In addition to the consequences for Bible-believing Christians, the restriction of religious liberty will have negative consequences for the entire nation. If the current trajectory is not reversed, one religion—Secular Progressivism—will be granted complete freedom in the public square while other religions will be barred from participation. And here's the irony—the day will come when the concerns of today's secular progressives will not reflect the concerns of *tomorrow's* cultural majority, and then it will be they—today's secular progressives—whose liberties will be curtailed. In denigrating religious liberty, they are happily building an enormous cannon, thinking only of their contemporary conservative targets. But one day the cannon will turn on them. The question is not *if* but *when.*

So what can ordinary folks like you and me do to help safeguard religious liberty? For one, vote for politicians who support it. (And keep an eye out: religious liberty isn't valued by everyone in either of our two major parties.) Beyond that, leverage the various opportunities you've got—coffee-shop conversations, blog posts, classroom debates—to make known that you support religious freedom in its fullest sense. Make the case with compassion and sympathy so that your detractors have no warrant to say that you're just being selfish.

Make the case that religion cannot be contained. It cannot be restricted to the private realm. Religious beliefs are heartfelt and personal, but precisely for that reason they also radiate outward into our speech and actions. This is true for people who worship the God of Jesus Christ or the Allah of Muhammad, for those who worship sex or money or power, and for those who worship at the altar of secular progressivism. Fight for the right of all people to exercise their religion (unless, of course, their "exercise" poses a clear and present danger to other citizens).

Make the case that true religion cannot be coerced. No single religion, whether Christianity or secular progressivism, should seek to force other-believers to fit in its mold. Just as the law shouldn't compel secular business owners to pay for their employees to receive biblical counseling, in the same way it shouldn't compel Christian business owners to pay for their employees' contraceptive abortifacients.

Make the case that religion cannot be replaced. Religion serves as the natural counterbalance to government. It alone has the heft to keep government in check, to prevent government from encroaching on every square inch of society and culture. Why do you think Russia, China, and Saudi Arabia are so nervous about religious liberty? As I see it, strong churches and healthy Christianity provide the best safeguard against authoritarianism.

And finally we should point out to the secular progressives that, if they are turned off by the excesses of the *Religious* Right, they should imagine the horrors of an ascendant *Irreligious* (read: Alt) Right. Cut off from the ultimacy of a just and authoritative God, secular societies are more—rather than less—prone to injustice. Religious liberty truly is necessary for the preservation of justice and freedom. We support religious liberty, fundamentally, because we love our neighbors.

Well, I'm going to sign off for now. Please say hello to Pastor Greean at Pinnacle Church. And don't hesitate to send your next query. You've kept up a pretty good pace during the spring semester. I hope I can keep up with what I imagine will be a torrential downpour of letters from you this summer, now that you are finished with exams and papers.

Yours, .
Bruce

THERE ARE NO SAFE SPACES IN THE REAL WORLD

Christian,

Thank you for your most recent letter, and congratulations on receiving your first writing assignment from CCNN! An opinion piece about the campus unrest at Queenstown Divinity School—sounds like a doozy!

As you requested, I'm happy to help you think through the issues. Let's start with the facts. Queenstown had invited an evangelical pastor to speak at chapel. Student activists demanded the school *rescind* their invitation. The pastor's crime? He believes historic Christian teaching about gender and sexuality. The administration's response? They agreed to the activist's demands.

Neither you nor I are especially surprised or impressed by this most recent iteration of the PC shuttering of free speech. In the past couple of years, college students have shouted down, pepper-sprayed, punched, and otherwise shut down the campus guests whose ideas they considered offensive. The most prominent recent cases have included Milo Yiannopoulos (Berkeley), Charles Murray (Middlebury College), and Heather MacDonald (Claremont McKenna), but a number of institutions have disinvited scheduled speakers and even disciplined students for expressing their ideas.

And those institutions are some of our nation's most prestigious. Brown University, Johns Hopkins, Williams, and other universities succumbed to student pressure by disinviting scheduled speakers whose views some students found offensive. William & Mary, the University of Colorado, and De Paul University disciplined students for criticizing affirmative action. The University of Kansas disciplined a professor for criticizing the National Rifle Association. Free speech seems to be having a tough time on college campuses these days.

So the Queenstown situation is a garden-variety instance of a much larger trend. That doesn't mean it doesn't have its own interesting aspects. For instance, did you see the television footage of the protest? Hands down, my favorite protester was the guy holding a protest sign while rollerblading in a toga. I mean, hey, at least there's one aspect of his life—fashion and accessories—in which he isn't in lockstep conformity with the PC agenda and its professional agitators. There was also the Queenstown professor whose moustache should've nabbed a nomination for Best Supporting Actor in this well-choreographed, "spontaneous" protest. But I digress.

You made a great point in your letter when you said concerned citizens are going to have to make a fresh case for the value of free speech. I couldn't agree more. If we can't make a convincing case for its value, this trend will continue indefinitely until free speech has been shuttered not only on university campuses but also in coffee shops, churches, and public squares. The prospect seems almost ludicrous. What could be more American than freedom of speech? And yet, here we are.

How in the world did we get here? More importantly, is there an exit off this self-destructive highway?

A couple of law professors at UC-Irvine, Erwin Chemerinsky and Howard Gillman, do a decent job explaining how we got here. In their recent research about free speech, they found that many of this generation's college students are simply acting out the beliefs that were given to them when they were young. Namely, that we should oppose bullies and protect others against intolerant or offensive speech. They aren't much impressed with legal precedents about free speech, being more concerned about defending the vulnerable. For many college students, then, "free speech" is an abstract right and one many of them are willing to discard, at times, in favor of other values.

To an audience like this, you may not find a hearing just by reminding them that free speech rights have always been embedded in our Constitution (which is true). After all, some instances of public speech are genuinely hateful and therefore deeply disturbing. Running back to "It's in the Constitution!" can sound insensitive, as if we're making light of the negative psychological impact of offensive and hateful speech. Better to appeal to your audience's better angels. If they're as concerned with protecting the vulnerable and marginalized as they claim, show them that protecting freedom of speech is *precisely* the way to do it. When we haphazardly curtail free speech, we hurt the very people we intend to protect.

Showing the practical negative consequences of restricting speech seems to be the wisest approach in today's context. So, for instance, you might point out that the restriction of free speech:

1. *Defeats the purpose of going to college in the first place.* One of the purposes of higher education is to welcome students of all backgrounds and teach them how to discuss and debate a wide variety of ideas. The restriction of free speech undermines that purpose. As much as some people may want to create a "safe space" in which offensive or controversial words have no place, that impulse runs contrary to the notion of academic inquiry. If you want a place where you aren't challenged by differing viewpoints, skip college and turn on the echo chamber of cable TV.

2. *Erodes the free and democratic nature of American society.* Public universities should serve as microcosms of democratic society. Michael Bloomberg and Charles Koch put it well: "The purpose of a college education isn't to reaffirm students' beliefs, it is to challenge, expand, and refine them—and to send students into the world with minds that are open and questioning, not closed and self-righteous. This helps young people discover their talents and prepare them for citizenship in a diverse, pluralistic democratic society. American society is not always a comfortable place to be; the college campus shouldn't be, either."[1]

3. *Encourages hypocrisy and undermines our ability to persuade.* If free speech is suppressed, you won't know who people really are. People who hold hateful or offensive views will hide who they are, and you'll never be able to persuade them of the wrongness of their views. You don't defeat bad ideas by hiding them but by refuting them.

4. *Ignores the fact that social progress often depends on free speech.* Many of the ideas most Americans

cherish—such as racial and gender equality—were once considered offensive. But they are no longer considered offensive precisely because courageous American citizens were allowed to display the merits of those ideas in public discussion and debate.

5. *Tilts our society in an authoritarian direction.* Suppression, no matter how well intentioned, breeds further suppression. If universities are free today to ban unintentionally offensive racial expressions, they will be free tomorrow to ban any sort of critique or evaluation of social groupings. As legal scholar Eugene Volokh has noted, Christians could be banned from criticizing tenets of Islam and vice versa. Pacifists could be restricted from criticizing the military. Conservatives could be disciplined for arguing that there are biological differences between men and women.[2] And those are just the trends we can anticipate. Ideological winds tend to change direction, so there's no telling what aspect of normative speech today may be considered inappropriate tomorrow. Students who are eager to suppress other people's speech may soon wake up to find their own speech being suppressed.

For Americans who are Christians, there is yet another reason to promote free speech: we want to be free to preach the Christian gospel even though many people find Christianity offensive and discriminatory. And if we do not stem the tide of free-speech restrictions, we might find ourselves in a situation one day where our nation's universities and public squares make it illegal to speak about that which is most precious to us. If that day comes, I pray that Christians will have the courage to exercise their *true* freedom in Christ, speaking the truth even in the face of legal consequences. As Peter and John said when they were told to muzzle their message, "We are unable to stop speaking about what we have seen and heard" (Acts 4:20). Before God we are always free—more than free, *compelled*—to speak the truth. But we shouldn't, therefore, neglect God's gift of a society that also allows it.

These things said, Christian, I want to return to a legitimate concern campus protesters have. Sometimes speakers say things that are not only offensive to the ears of the listener but genuinely wrong and worthy of being rebuked. Given that concern, you should offer some alternatives.

For example, if students are offended by the views of a guest speaker, they can use social media to encourage other students not to attend. Or they can hold a parallel event in which they rebut the speaker's ideas. Still another option is to attend the scheduled event, listen to the speaker present his offensive views, and then—gasp!—use the Q&A time to raise questions about the speaker's errant views.

As for professors, you should encourage them to foster a classroom environment in which students are exposed to new ideas, learn to evaluate those ideas, and, when necessary, criticize those ideas. In other words, a professor should be more like a professor than a member of the thought police.

As for administrators, why not write a letter to the university's top administrators, asking them to make good policies against mob shout downs and beat downs and then enforce those policies? I'm not sure there is much hope for many of them. But they certainly won't change anything if we just stay silent. And I've seen some recent trends that seem promising.

In fact, in response to recent trends curtailing free speech, the University of Chicago sent out a letter to incoming students, affirming its commitment to freedom of inquiry and expression. "Our commitment to academic freedom," dean of students John Ellison wrote, "means that we do not support so-called 'trigger warnings,' we do not cancel invited speakers because their topics might prove controversial, and we do not condone the creation of intellectual 'safe spaces' where individuals can retreat from ideas and perspectives at odds with their own."[3] Well put.

Ellison went on to affirm that "fostering the free exchange of ideas reinforces a related university priority—building a campus that welcomes people of all backgrounds. Diversity of opinion and background is a fundamental strength of our community. The members of our community must have the freedom to espouse and explore a wide range of ideas."

Kudos to the University of Chicago, one of our nation's premier universities, for doing the right thing. They've faced some severe criticism for it, and I wouldn't be surprised if they saw a dip in tuition and donor revenue. Considering the value of free speech, it's a price worth paying.

As wrong as those who oppose free speech appear to be, we'll gain nothing by treating them with cynicism or condescension. Sometimes they have legitimate concerns, and we can learn a lot from them. They may recognize harmful ideologies or hateful attitudes before we do, and why would we ignore that?

As followers of Christ, we should have as strong a distaste for hateful speech as anyone, *especially* when it is directed toward those who are vulnerable. We should be concerned about the psychological impact hateful speech has on its victims. We should encourage our universities to create teaching and learning environments that foster civility, respect, and brotherly love. In many ways, we can stand shoulder to shoulder with the protestors in fighting for a world where our words are used to bless and heal rather than to curse and destroy.

And yet, we must not curtail offensive speech by shuttering civil liberties. To do so would invite even worse social ills, such as a society that is increasingly authoritarian, a university that doesn't challenge its students, and a people who hide who they really are.

I'm proud of you, Christian, and I'm confident your opinion piece for CCNN will be a winner. I'm pulling for you as you play a role in supporting America's constitutional vision for a free society and the university's role as a place that strengthens the student body's ability to ask honest questions and give honest answers rather than becoming professional billboard holders and shout-down artists.

I'll happily take credit for any praise your article receives. And if you receive any strong criticism, I'll assume you didn't listen to my advice here. Such is the privilege of being the dispenser of wisdom.

Just kidding.

Sorta.

You responded to my last letter in world-record time—thirty minutes after I wrote you. From the way you're framing your questions, I can tell that you've moved from being merely a "political junkie" to being a concerned *Christian* American. That's encouraging. I'll tell you what: you get to work on your free speech article, and I'll get to work addressing our next topic for conversation—abortion.

Yours,

Bruce

CHAPTER 10

UNBORN LIVES MATTER

Christian,

I saw your fantastic op-ed about free speech being fundamental for social progress. Congrats. And an even more hearty congratulation for inciting a small protest at the CCNN offices in Manhattan! Several dozen protestors, if I can trust the reports I've heard. Nice work! I think you struck a nerve—in a good way.

I noticed that the protesters held signs accusing you of being a "hater" because you want to protect the right of hateful people to speak their minds in public. Guilt by association, I suppose. I wonder if the protestors really believe that, though. You never really know, as many of these protests are orchestrated by professional agitators who are trying to score social and political points. You'd have to share a cup of coffee with the protestors to figure out if they really believe what they were shouting at you.

Nonetheless, you did the right thing. You wrote a solid opinion piece that defends free speech in public places and thereby safeguards the free and democratic nature of our republic. That a piece defending free speech is required saddens my heart; that many still *are* defending free speech gives me a smidgen of hope.

Speaking of safeguarding the free and democratic nature of our republic (justice and liberty for all!), our next topic for discussion is abortion. When you wrote last, you mentioned that you'll be taking a course in "reproductive rights" at Dupont in the fall.

"Reproductive rights." That's an interesting phrase, isn't it? It makes it sound as if the faculty at Dupont want to protect a woman's right to have children—a "right to repro-duce." That may not be a coherent right—a person having the "right to reproduce" makes just as little sense as having the "right" to be six feet tall or the "right" to be born into money; but as you know, that isn't how the phrase is used.

The phrase is used by people whose concern is not to protect women's rights to have as many babies as they wish without their lovers or parents forcing them to take the babies' lives in the womb. Instead, their concern is to allow women to end the lives of their unborn children. It's not about the freedom to reproduce without interference but the freedom to participate in reproductive activity (i.e., sex) without consequence. The whole business of "reproductive rights" is a handy linguistic camouflage intended to prevent people from having to talk about "termination rights." But I imagine Termination Rights 201 isn't as easy on the eyes when one reads the fall semester's course catalog.

Let me take a moment to explore the progressive notion of reproductive freedom and to define some terms such as *abortion, embryo, human,* and *person.* What exactly is the freedom being used for, and what choice is being made? As I've already mentioned, we are nearly always referring to the woman's freedom to have an abortion.

An *abortion* is the termination of a pregnancy that leads to the death of an embryo or fetus and its expulsion from the womb. Medically speaking, any pregnancy that results in the child's death is classified as an abortion, regardless of the means (this would include miscarriages). Because of this broad definition, many people find it helpful to clarify that the issue at stake is *elective* abortion—i.e., a woman choosing to end a fetus's life. Most people, though, when they hear "abortion," think predominantly of "elective abortion."

The term *embryo* is used to refer to a developing human from the time of implantation to the end of the eighth week after conception, while the term *fetus* is used to refer to an unborn or unhatched vertebrate, specifically a developing human from two months after conception to birth.[1]

The distinction between an embryo and a fetus is rather synthetic and can often confuse people as they're considering the morality of abortion. Because of that, I'll simply use the terms "unborn human being" or "unborn being" to refer to *either* a human embryo or a fetus at any stage from conception to birth. As you'll see, the arguments are not substantively different whether the unborn is six weeks or six months along.

What exactly is this unborn human being? Let's survey the options: it could be one of four things: part, parasite, property, or person.

I have heard some people with particular pluck claim that the unborn being is a *part* of the woman's body. They claim that an abortion is similar to clipping a woman's toenails. This claim runs counter to common sense and counter to scientific consensus. Think about it. Every part of a woman's body—including her toenail clippings—contains *her* unique DNA. But the unborn being has its own unique

DNA. Therefore, the unborn being cannot be a part of the woman's body.

Another claim, made famous by the philosopher Judith Jarvis Thomson, contends that the unborn being is essentially a *parasite* that feeds off the mother's body.[2] Thompson argues that the mother has a right to decide what happens to her body and that the mother's "right to choose" trumps the unborn being's right to live. So at least there's an admission that we're dealing with something *living.* One of the key problems with this, however, is that a parasite is something that attaches itself to a host and feeds on it for survival; the embryo or fetus does not attach itself to the mother's womb but is created by the mother and father in the mother's womb. Another problem is that the same logic can be used to justify infanticide. Newborns feed off their mother's body, but hardly anyone makes the argument that mothers have the right to kill their children until they are weaned.

Most people, even pro-choice advocates, recognize that the unborn being is neither a part nor a parasite of the women. What about *property*? Surprisingly, this is how the legal system treats the unborn. When the Supreme Court case *Roe v. Wade* legalized abortion, the justices appealed to the Fourteenth Amendment's "Due Process clause," which says the state cannot deprive a person of life, liberty, or property without due process.

The court was saying in *Roe* that state abortion laws like the one in Texas were depriving women of a basic liberty protected by the Due Process Clause. But what sort of liberty is the right of abortion? As we've noted, the unborn being is not a part of the woman's body. And as we'll see, the court also makes clear they do not consider the unborn to be a person. So the "liberty" being offered to the woman is the freedom to treat the unborn being as her personal property or what the law would consider "personalty," that is a movable asset (goods, chattel, things, things whether animate or inanimate as opposed to "real property" (land)).[3]

Is the unborn human being really considered the property of the mother? Do Americans still think it's OK for one human being to own another?

Yes, many Americans do. Or at least they pretend to. Under *Roe*, the unborn being is treated as property to which the woman has almost exclusive rights. The state can only interfere with these rights when they have a compelling interest and then only after the first trimester. Until that time the woman has the right to "dispose" of her property in any manner she chooses.

Christian, this is deeply ironic, especially in a nation such as the United States, which claims to have left slavery in the dust of distant history. There is no other situation in which an American can legally own another human being, much less choose whether or not to terminate the human person they "own." To get around this problem, the Supreme Court makes a distinction that most people wouldn't understand: they claim that the unborn *human being* is not a *person*.

I know, I know. You're thinking, *How in the world do you say that someone is a living human being but isn't a person? Isn't that an a=a situation?*

Sadly, no. Historically there have often been groups of humans who were not considered people. In many cases slaves, women, infants, Jews, or "foreigners" were all, at one time or another, denied legal or moral standing as *persons*, despite being recognized as *humans*. Happily, in recent years America as a society has determined it is evil to deny personhood to human beings.

Unless, of course, that human being happens to be in utero. Supposedly, those little humans aren't persons.

Is there a logically consistent way of defining *person-hood* that doesn't include all human beings? What might that rubric for personhood look like? It depends on whom you ask. Not surprisingly, when you allow secular intellectuals and philosophers to define *personhood*, they will attempt to establish a criterion based on intellect, reason, and consciousness. Ethicist Joseph Fletcher, for example, believed a human with an IQ below forty might not be a person, and those with an IQ below twenty are *definitely* not persons. Princeton philosopher Peter Singer believes that since patients with Alzheimer's and infants up to the age of twenty-four months are not persons (he uses similar reasoning for his definitions), it is not wrong to kill them.

Of course, the standards these philosophers put in place can be used to justify killing *them* too. For instance, every night these philosophers fall into a state of prolonged unconsciousness, whereby they would no longer under their definition classify as "people." We call it "sleep." And we all agree that you can't just kill philosophers in their sleep. Even the nasty ones.

The entire hairsplitting discussion about what makes a human being a person ignores a point that forms the basis of *our* entire argument: all human beings—whether we consider them persons or nonpersons—are made in the image of God.

Now I'm about to get theological for a moment. And I know that most of your friends won't accept it. So before I dive into the theological reasons abortion is wrong, I want briefly to outline an argument you *can* use with your friends. It's what Scott Klusendorf calls the SLED method.[4] This helpfully takes the discussion away from the nuances of "human being" or "person" and simply tries to show that the unborn are not fundamentally different from *us*. These are the only four differences between the unborn and you:

- *S—Size.* Unborn humans are smaller than us. But it's bananas to say that smaller humans have less value. A guy wearing an XL T-shirt isn't somehow three times as important as a petite woman.
- *L—Level of development.* Unborn humans are less developed than mature adults. But so are toddlers. For that matter, so are teenagers. Recognizing a human's lower level of development (in the young) usually leads us to foster development, not to impair it.
- *E—Environment.* The unborn are in the womb, and the rest of us aren't. Legally, this is a huge deal for abortion rights. But does the location of a human change their value in any other instance? Is a woman at her office in Manhattan more valuable than a young man, say, at a Dupont basketball game?
- *D—Degree of dependency.* Unborn humans need their mothers to survive. But again, since when do we think that *need* implies lower *value?* If your friend drinks too much and passes out in a pool, his degree of dependency suddenly skyrockets. Your response, we would hope, would be to *help* him, not to assume he isn't fit for life.

OK, back to the Bible. For us Christians, we have *even more* reason to oppose abortion.

God created human beings in his own image and likeness (Gen. 1:26) and knows unborn human beings intimately and individually just as he knows adults. As King David said to God, "For it was you who created my inward parts; you knit me together in my mother's womb. I will praise you because I have been remarkably and wondrously made" (Ps. 139:13–14). Notice that he identified himself, an adult human being, with the same being that was unborn. David understood that he was not a mere part of his mother's body, nor was he knit-ted together as a parasite. Being created by God, David was not property to be disposed of at the whim of his mother. And whether he was recognized as a person, he was recognized by God, in whose image he was made (Gen. 5:1).

God consecrates babies for special service even while they are in the womb (Luke 1:41), considers a baby's life equally valuable as an adult's life (Exod. 21:22–25), com-mands us not to kill innocent human beings (Exod. 20:13), and loves humanity enough that he sent his own Son to die to save us from our sins (John 3:16).

Your friends may not be convinced by the biblical evi-dence. They might shrug their shoulders at Klusendorf's SLED analogy. But your friends probably care about protect-ing the vulnerable. So I want to conclude this mammoth letter with a few sociological reasons that elective abortion hurts all of us. There are eight major reasons.[5]

1. *Abortion hurts the baby.* Dying in violent and ago-nizing manner, somewhere between one and two million innocent baby humans are killed each year. Not everyone agrees whether these humans are people, but everyone agrees that they feel pain. This is one reason pro-abortionists resort to socially neu-tral euphemisms such as "products of conception" and "termination of pregnancy." As the authors of "The America We Seek" note, "The unborn child in America today enjoys less legal protection than an endangered species of bird in a national forest."

2. *Abortion hurts women.* Our country's legalization of abortion damages women by communicating to them that it is morally and legally acceptable to take the life of their baby. This legalization has catalyzed male irresponsibility and predatory sexual behavior that,

in turn, destabilizes romantic relationships and marriages. The process of abortion itself leaves women with long-term emotional and psychological damage, even for those who eagerly approached abortion beforehand.

3. *Abortion hurts men.* Abortion on demand means many fathers must watch as their children are killed against their will; some months, years, or even decades later, fathers find out that the child they would've wanted to nurture was killed without their input or consent.

4. *Abortion hurts marriages and families.* Abortion hurts families in numerous ways, among which are: its destruction of a baby, fueling of male irresponsibility, marginalization of fatherhood, and the implicit message that if people in our lives cause us problems, then those people literally *are* problems and not even people. No wonder the United States experiences so much lethal violence.

5. *Abortion undermines justice and equality.* Abortion should not be a matter of choice any more than other situations that involve taking the life of an innocent person. When we allow our citizens to attack the most vulnerable group of human beings in our society, we undermine our nation's claim to being a law-governed democracy. No longer does our nation really believe we are *all* created equal; no longer do we seek justice for *all.*

6. *Abortion undermines our nation's system of checks and balances.* In *Roe v. Wade* and subsequent decisions, the Supreme Court majority bypassed democratic debate and legislation by fabricating a constitutional right to abortion. Even today, for instance, support for

late-term abortion is incredibly low (less than 20 percent); but many political activists continue to press for greater access to abortion and fewer restrictions.

7. *Abortion minimizes society's mediating institutions.* Abortion on demand assumes an individual (the mother) has the right to take a life without the consent of the baby's father or siblings. This sort of individual autonomy pushes America even further toward a cultural environment where the only actors of consequence are the ever-expanding state and the solitaire individual.

8. *Abortion hurts society at large.* In an article supporting the pro-life movement, Harvard law professor Mary Ann Glendon wrote, "There is growing awareness that the moral ecology of the country has suffered something like an environmental disaster, and that we are faced with a very complicated clean-up operation."[6] Indeed, abortion license has eroded the moral foundations of our civic community and numbed our collective consciences by normalizing lethal violence against innocent humans. Instead of reinforcing our intuitive desire to protect those persons among us who are weakest and most vulnerable, it demands that we adjust our consciences to the termination of those persons. To use biblical language, we are slowly searing our own consciences.

Christian, you've recently become a Christian, and you've embarked on an extended project of rethinking your political commitments and policy stances. I hope you'll place the protection of innocent human life at the top of your list of political commitments.

More to the point, I hope your concern will ultimately be rooted in the gospel of Christ. Abortion leaves a trail of destruction and pain, but the gospel provides an answer. The gospel speaks a healing word to the millions of men and women who have abortion as part of *their* story. To women who have walked through abortion, the gospel tells of a Son who died to liberate us from residual guilt. To men who approved of or pressured others into an abortion, the gospel tells of a Father who, rather than crushing us when we deserved it, allowed his heart to be crushed as he extended his arms of love to us. And to doctors whose hands have been employed in abortive procedures, the gospel introduces a Great Physician who offers eternal life, even for those who have caused temporal death.

Yours,
Bruce

CHAPTER 11

BLACK LIVES MATTER

Christian,

I should have warned you. Yes, it *is* normal to receive hate mail for days and even weeks after you've written an opinion piece for a national news outlet. Don't let it bother you. You've done a great job being even-keeled and even gracious in light of the unfair and inaccurate accusations that have been lobbed your way. Try to remember that for every inflammatory bomb launched into your in-box, there are probably hundreds or thousands of people who were enriched and encouraged by what you had to say. (They just tend to be less vocal.)

Back to business: I'm glad, though hardly surprised, that we're on the same page about abortion on demand. Our freedoms in the United States should not include taking the lives of innocent unborn human beings. Unborn lives matter. Speaking of which, it's time to talk about the Black Lives Matter movement.

You're right that a pro-life ethic is not worth its salt unless it values every life from womb to tomb. We pro-lifers should be willing to speak on behalf of born lives as well as unborn, black lives as well as white, Americans as well as citizens of other nations. When liberals critique the conservative pro-life cause for being inconsistent, they too often have decent material to work with.

In an environment like this, it's tempting to want to jump on a bandwagon with the label, Black Lives Matter (BLM). After all, *black lives do matter*. And yet you've expressed no small amount of nervousness with BLM as a movement. I think your summary statement hits the mark rather well: "If Black Lives Matter meant 'black lives matter,' I'd be all for it. But it seems to mean something more." Touché.

Before I discuss BLM directly, let me back up a bit. I want to survey the prominent American views on racism and how to overcome each, evaluating them in light of Christian teaching. Too often Christians tend to buy in thoughtlessly to secular models (offered to us by our favorite cable news networks), assuming their compatibility with Christianity. But we should be careful when riding waves before we know the tides that caused them.

None of the secular models are entirely compatible with our faith. George Yancey, a black sociologist at the University of North Texas, does a good job summarizing the current secular approaches in his book *Beyond Racial Gridlock*.[1] He reveals the flaws in America's two dominant *definitions* of racism and its four dominant *models* for overcoming racism. If you're tired of my letters and you have plenty of time on your hands, you can skip the rest of this letter and just read his book.

Assuming you're still with me . . .

First, the two dominant definitions of racism. One flawed view of racism views it as an entirely *individual* phenomenon, something that is only done by one individual to another. White evangelicals tend to adopt this definition because evangelical theology has a strong concept of personal sin. Thus, if a sin problem exists (and racism certainly qualifies), it must necessarily occur on the individual level.

Conversely, another flawed view focuses on the way racial sin and prejudice warp our society's cultural institutions, sometimes minimizing individual responsibility. This makes systemic racism the definition of racism proper. As you may have experienced anecdotally, black Americans are more likely than white Americans to adopt this posture.

A problem with both of these views is that often their proponents ignore the full spiritual and theological dimensions of race and racism. For that reason each view overemphasizes a particular side of the individual/structural coin. Scripture teaches that sin is committed by individuals, but it also teaches that our sin corrupts and misdirects social and cultural institutions. We should hardly be surprised to find racism both in individuals and in structures.

Second, the four dominant models for overcoming racism:

1. *The first model is colorblindness.* Proponents of this view think the best way to overcome racism is to ignore it, to see beyond the differences between the races. Christians are often drawn to this view because they recognize that humans are defined primarily by their relationship to God rather than by their ethnic heritage. The strength of this model is that it wants to stop individuals from being personally prejudiced, and it helps persons of color to avoid looking for racism where it does not exist. One weakness of this model is that it ignores the Bible's positive emphasis on human diversity; the culmination of human history does not include a multitude of clear people too great to number but a multitude too great to number from every tribe, tongue, and nation.

Another weakness is that it ignores or minimizes the Bible's teaching that sin—including racism and racial injustice—corrupts and misdirects social and cultural institutions. If institutions are made of individuals, and individuals are sinful even in ways they are not aware of, we can expect our institutions will sometimes and in some ways embody and propagate racism.

2. *The second model is Anglo conformity.* Proponents of this view think racism and racial tension will be resolved when persons of color gain the sort of upward mobility that many whites have. In other words, they think racial problems are primarily economic. As such, the solutions tend toward government-sponsored programs for the poor. The strength of this model is that it acknowledges tough economic realities and looks for minorities to take the lead in solving the ills of their families and neighborhoods. One weakness of this model is that it places too much emphasis on economic solutions. Another is that it doesn't place enough emphasis on the ways racism manifests itself in social and cultural institutions. Just ask any wealthy African-American if his financial status has exempted him from experiences of racism.

3. *The third model is relativistic multiculturalism.* Proponents of this view want to build a society that caters to distinct racial and ethnic groups. They want diversity present in public schools, official government forms, and political party platforms. The strength of this model is that it respects individual racial and ethnic groups and encourages members of those groups to celebrate their own cultures. The greatest

weakness of this model, however, is the way it tends to relativize "right" and "wrong" by allowing minority cultures to go uncritiqued. Multiculturalism generally affirms culture *qua* culture, overlooking the fact that elements of *every* culture are warped and sinful.

4. *The fourth model is white responsibility.* Advocates for this view rightly place the blame for America's historic racism squarely on whites. In certain American colleges "critical race theory" adopts the white-responsibility view but goes further, arguing that racism is inherent to American culture. The strength of this model is its revelation of the ways a single group can dominate social groupings and cultural institutions. The problem with this model is that it sometimes ignores sins committed by minorities and in so doing ironically disempowers minorities by alleviating them of responsibility while at the same time alienating whites.

So much for the four secular models. Each of them is flawed, and we—Christian Americans—need to find a more constructive path forward. Our worldview gives us a unique position to offer legitimate assessment *and* hope in our racially charged times. Consider, for instance, the relevance of three core Christian doctrines:

1. *Creation.* The Bible teaches that God designed the world as a beautiful unity in diversity. God created each unique person in his image and likeness, endowing us with great dignity and value (Gen. 1:27–28). This fact alone should cause a Christian to work hard to repent of his personal prejudices and to reshape any cultural institutions that put persons of color at a disadvantage.

2. *Sin.* The Bible makes clear that all sin, including racism, is manifested at the individual and cultural levels and that its roots go much deeper than we initially realize. It's not enough to encourage individuals to repent of their prejudices; nor can we expect a purely structural solution to eradicate the persistent sin that festers in *every one* of our hearts. The reality of sin should also make us less squeamish to call out elements of America's past that have been shaped by racism. Nations, as well as individuals, are bound up in the complicated paradox of both God-given beauty and Satan-influenced sin.

3. *Salvation.* The Bible teaches that God sent his brown, Aramaic-speaking, Middle Eastern Son, Jesus, to save us from our sins and restore our unity with one another. "There is no Jew or Greek, slave or free, male and female; since you are all one in Christ Jesus" (Gal. 3:28). Jesus will put this unity on full display when he returns one day to gather people of all ethnic and cultural heritages together before his throne. This unified worship will not destroy racial distinctions but will destroy racial supremacy and racial sin once and for all. The practical takeaway is that when Christians display racial unity, it serves as a "preview" of Christ's future kingdom.

Once we establish that God's great love is for persons of every ethnic and cultural heritage, we realize that our pro-life ethic must value every life—black, white, or otherwise—from the time they're in their mother's womb to the moment they're dropped in the ground. So yes, let's say it loud and clear: *Black lives matter.*

Isn't that the end of it? Shouldn't we just sign our names onto the Black Lives Matter movement and be done with it? Not so fast.

I'm not sure if you remember, Christian, but BLM began as a social media protest against George Zimmerman's acquittal after he shot and killed Trayvon Martin (a young black man). Three black community activists—Alicia Garza, Patrisse Cullors, and Opal Tometi—used the hashtag #blacklivesmatter on Twitter to question the legitimacy of Zimmerman's acquittal. The hashtag stuck. When two other black men—Michael Brown and Eric Garner—were subsequently killed by police officers, the hashtag reemerged as a social media rallying cry.

Assessing the meaning of a hashtag is harder than you might think. One of the biggest difficulties in assessing BLM is that the talking heads on television each have their own agenda. Shocking, right? And in lieu of a firm definition, they tend to spin things the way they want the story to go, either describing BLM in an entirely positive manner (to promote it) or in an across-the-board negative way (to decry it). You've seen this predictable song and dance, I'm sure.

Another difficulty lies in the fact that BLM is a grassroots organization with decentralized leadership. Its many loosely affiliated groups and activists differ from one another in their agendas and methodology. So even an evenhanded news agency would have a difficult time defining the contours of BLM.

In spite of those challenges, we can describe some of the core principles shared by *most* BLM groups and activists. BLM groups and leaders tend to coalesce around their affirmation of cultural diversity in general and America's black and LGBTQ communities in particular. (That latter association surprised me too at first. More on that in a moment.) Politically, they articulate their goals in terms of ending the war on black people, seeking reparations, investing in education for the black community, seeking economic justice, and gaining independent black political power.

So, that is an extremely concise summary of BLM. As we begin to evaluate BLM, Christian, it will be helpful for you to "clear the decks" mentally by rejecting some of the caricatures you might have bought into. On the one hand, your Uncle John dismisses BLM as a worthless movement that is violent to the core and in which nothing good can be found. On the other hand, your professors tend to affirm comprehensively any type of campus activist groups (with the notable exception of groups who promote historic Christianity). Both approaches—mindless dismissal and uncritical embrace—are wrong.

Mika Edmonson, a black Presbyterian pastor, has written a helpful little article about BLM titled, "Is Black Lives Matters the New Civil Rights Movement?"[2] I think he's got the right approach, which I'll try to summarize here (while also drawing on two other African-American public intellectuals, Anthony Bradley and Jason Riley).

As I've said already, we must affirm, vocally and with conviction, that black lives matter. This affirmation does not come from a vacuum but has become necessary as, over the past few years, a number of black men have been shot to death by white police officers, leaving many black Americans not only frustrated and angry but also *afraid*. They are afraid that "justice and equality for all" doesn't apply to their sons. They are afraid to let their sons go outside at night for fear a routine traffic stop could spell the end of their life.

As Christians, we should be the first to weep with those who weep. We don't have to act as the judge or jury of any particular police officer, or of police officers in general, in order to sympathize and show genuine Christian love to black friends and neighbors who are grieving, angry, or afraid. When we weep with those who weep, we tend to open up as human beings. We see things in a way we didn't see them before. We have the opportunity to correct our misperceptions. This sort of humility is in very short supply in America's polarized and toxic public square, and it would be an ugly irony if we followers of Jesus (Jesus, who humbled himself for our sake) are not able to muster some openness and humility.

And we can affirm some aspects of BLM as a movement, too. As Edmonson points out, our affirmations of BLM will tend to be in areas where BLM aligns with the Civil Rights Movement (CRM) of the 1960s. We agree with BLM, for instance, that Americans should work to end any injustices toward black persons and communities. Regarding tactics, we can affirm that most BLM leaders and activists want to reveal injustice through nonviolent action rather than violence and militancy.

Our criticisms of BLM will tend to be in areas where BLM departs from CRM. BLM rejects the Christian roots and aims of the CRM. As a whole, BLM implicitly rejects the Christian gospel, while many of its affiliated groups and activists explicitly reject it. That is why Anthony Bradley wrote, "Christians need not employ any number of creative hermeneutics to attempt to theologically justify it [BLM], make it consistent with Christianity, or explain their proximity to it."[3]

BLM also departs from CRM in terms of it organizing cases. Whereas the CRM highlighted "perfect victim" cases, which could tip social climates in the favor of their movement (think Rosa Parks, an elderly and vulnerable female, refusing to give up her seat on a bus), BLM "organize(s) around what critics might call 'morally ambiguous cases.'"[4] (Think videos of black males being shot by white police officers. While we often do not have broader context to determine the guilt or innocence of the black male, BLM "insist(s) that no one should be tried, convicted, and executed on the street.")[5]

CRM aside, there are other problems with BLM. Significantly, it promotes a deeply flawed model for economic justice. As Jason Riley notes, BLM doesn't sufficiently consider the reasons for the injustice they wish to address, and further, they fail to make proposals that will actually improve the situation.[6] Raising awareness can only go so far. Instead of relying on greater expansion of welfare systems, for instance, BLM activists should focus their efforts on what should be the role of the private sector—namely, seeking to bring jobs into poor neighborhoods and developing ways to support schools and education efforts.

I could go on. But I'll stop for now. One more thing, though, before I sign off: white conservative evangelical Christians need to stop burying our heads in the sand when it comes to racism and racial injustice. Even though we have serious and irreconcilable differences with BLM as a movement, we—as Bible-believing Christians—should have more motivation than anybody to fight racism and racial injustice wherever we find it. Historically, our record in this arena has been shamefully inconsistent (to put it kindly). I don't want us to spend too long flagellating ourselves for it, but I do want to see us put a new foot forward. It's time to fight racism tooth and nail not only from the pulpit but also in private conversations and in the public square. People of color deserve it, and our God demands it.

I hope your summer continues to go well. I'm looking forward to hearing your response to the ideas I've laid out in this letter.

Yours,

Bruce

CHAPTER 12

NOBODY THROWS A TANTRUM LIKE A POLITICALLY CORRECT AMERICAN

Christian,

Welcome to the big leagues! You got hammered from the Left when you wrote your pro-life opinion piece. And now you're being hammered from the fever swamps of the distant Right because you dared to mention the reality of racial injustice. It seems you've violated the PC norms of two different special interest groups. Take heart: even though the bulldogs of both sides won't rest, they'll soon find some other fresh meat to gnaw on.

Let's take some time to talk about political correctness itself—how it started, where it's headed, and how we should respond.

In order to address the politically correct norms that govern public discourse today, we have to return to a subject we discussed already—free speech. You're not old enough to remember the birth of the Free Speech Movement, so you wouldn't know that it was born on the campus of the University of California at Berkley in 1964. Come to think of it, I'm not old enough to remember it either.

Anyway, back in the sixties, one of Berkley's graduate students, Jack Weinberg, defied a campus-wide ban on political activism by setting up a table with political information. When police detained him, a group of approximately three thousand students surrounded the police car in which Weinberg was held, preventing it from moving for thirty-six hours. That event was the first mass civil disobedience of its sort on a college campus, and it led to similar protests across the country.

Berkley has every right to be proud of the Free Speech Movement. But now, fifty years later, the birthplace of the Free Speech Movement has become a hotbed for the suppression of speech. It turns out that the children and grandchildren of the original campus protestors aren't enamored with free speech unless it's speech they agree with. As I mentioned in an earlier letter, several speakers have been harassed and threatened for attempting to speak at the school. The Free Speech Movement has morphed into something a bit more insidious—political correctness. Cross one of the lines this crew deems important, and you'll know it. Do it consistently, and you may want to adopt a pseudonym or write from a secure and undisclosed location.

Now don't get me wrong. I said it earlier, and I'll say it again. We've got to disagree with bad ideas. We've got to confront the proponents of bad ideas by refuting their ideas. In short, we've got to do everything in our power to make bad ideas *look bad*. But we shouldn't oppose bad ideas by gagging the people who have those ideas. It's neither effective nor democratic.

In a 1906 book, *The Friends of Voltaire*, the English writer Evelyn Beatrice Hall put it this way: "I disapprove of what you say, but I will defend to the death your right to say it."[1] And for decades this view reigned among conservatives and liberals. In 1978, for example, the American Civil Liberties Union (ACLU) defended a small group of neo-Nazis who had planned a rally in Skokie, Illinois. The ACLU, in case you aren't aware, does not have much sympathy for neo-Nazis. In fact, it would be difficult to imagine two more different groups. But they defended the neo-Nazis' right to articulate their ideas. Today, however, many powerful progressive organizations have done a U-turn. They defend free speech in certain instances but not in others.

This brings us to a related topic—tolerance. Christian, you were right to ask how a Bible-believing Christian should view tolerance and whether we should be tolerant of hateful people. Sorta. I suspect that tolerance, which used to have an obvious and helpful meaning, is becoming nearly nonsensical. So I try to use different terms these days. I often say we should show Christian *love* toward people at the same time we *refute* their errant views. Love and refutation are better than *toleration*, whatever that means at the current hour.

I would love to see a reasonable definition of tolerance make a comeback. Tolerance itself is built on the foundation of a historic and Christian view of the relationship between truth and personal identity. In the online journal *Public Discourse*, Ben Crenshaw put it this way:

> The traditional understanding of tolerance reflects a certain epistemology: namely, that there is such a thing as truth, it can be known, and the best way to discover the truth is through debate, reflection, and investigation. The pursuit of truth requires mutual cooperation, serious consideration of opposing beliefs,

and persuasion through the use of reason. Coercion, exclusion, slander, and threats of force have no place in the search for truth.[2]

Today, however, many Americans reject this historic view. Instead they think truth is subjective and equated with personal identity. And if their beliefs are equated with their personal identity, any person who criticizes their beliefs is, in fact, criticizing *them* and should be considered a hateful person. It used to be that you could only *tolerate* a person you disagreed with. But these days, to disagree *is* to hate.

For example, if a Bible-believing Christian expresses the historic Christian view of marriage and sexual morality and if he articulates biblical restrictions on sexual activity outside the bounds of marriage between one man and one woman, the Christian is viewed as a "hateful bigot." The politically correct tolerance regime is incredibly intolerant; it wishes to crush all dissent by calling it "hate" or "bigotry."

We shouldn't tolerate this backwards view of tolerance. We should always show Christian love to members of the tolerance regime, but we should refute their flawed view of truth and identity. We should "speak the truth, each one to his neighbor" (Eph. 4:25) and refute ideas or beliefs that contradict the Word of God (1 Tim. 6:3), all while respecting them and showing Christian love to them. We have the opportunity to show people how to disagree *without despising our ideological opponent*, a combination many today think impossible.

The free speech and tolerance controversies relate directly to "political correctness," or, as it is often put, "the PC agenda." Many Americans enforce their intolerant toleration on society by creating and enforcing codes of political correctness.

You might be interested to know that the notion of political correctness first came into use among communists in the 1930s. The phrase was a (sometimes) humorous reminder that the party's interest is to be treated as a reality that ranks above reality itself. *("Comrade, your statement is factually incorrect." "Yes, it is. But it is politically correct.")*[3]

What started out as a subversive Soviet joke has become a humorless American reality. In the United States to be politically correct means to avoid any type of speech or action that dissents from secular orthodoxy, particularly in regards to the beliefs or lifestyles of persons who may be considered disadvantaged or socially marginalized. To exacerbate matters, the rise of identity politics has caused nearly every group in society to identify as socially disadvantaged or discriminated against in some way. Being aggrieved is the new cool.

I know you're busy, but I suggest you take the time to read a great little article, "On Political Correctness" by Professor William Deresiewicz. In it he describes his experience teaching at a small college in California:

> I had one student, from a Chinese-American family, who informed me that the first thing she learned when she got to college was to keep quiet about her Christian faith and her non-feminist views about marriage. I had another student, a self-described "strong feminist," who told me that she tends to keep quiet about everything, because she never knows when she might say something that you're not supposed to. I had a third student, a junior, who wrote about a friend whom she had known since the beginning of college and who, she'd just discovered, went to church every Sunday. My student hadn't even been aware that her friend was religious. When she asked her why she had concealed this essential fact about

herself, her friend replied, "Because I don't feel comfortable being out as a religious person here."[4]

Based on experiences such as this, Deresiewicz argues that most of America's elite schools function like seminaries. The only difference is that the dogma they are passing along is not a historic world religion but a contemporary code of permissions and prohibitions. We are told what we should be thinking and talking about and the right way to talk and think about those things. We are told what we should *always* do and what we must *never* do.

At the dead center of the moral code are issues of identity:

> Issues of identity—principally the holy trinity of race, gender, and sexuality—occupy the center of concern. The presiding presence is Michel Foucault, with his theories of power, discourse, and the social construction of the self, who plays the same role on the left as Marx once did. The fundamental questions that a college education ought to raise—questions of individual and collective virtue, of what it means to be a good person and a good community—are understood to have been settled. The assumption, on elite college campuses, is that we are already in full possession of the moral truth. This is a religious attitude. It is certainly not a scholarly or intellectual attitude.[5]

These cultural elites set up a standard for orthodox belief and excommunicate anyone who advocates "heretical" beliefs that are outside the accepted politically correct doctrine. Berkeley may not think of itself as a religious school. But you'd probably have a better time of it dealing with the Spanish Inquisition.

For me, the bottom line is this: today's codes of political correctness usually demand obeisance to progressive social norms that often conflict with our religious and political beliefs. For Bible-believing Christians, today's political correctness often demands social conformity at the expense of personal beliefs. It causes us either to be hypocrites about what we believe or to change certain aspects of our belief system, which, in turn, undercuts our ability to put our true beliefs to work for the common good.

What we need is not the dogmatic virulence of political correctness but the respect and decency of public *civility*. Civility encourages us to articulate our beliefs but to do so in a way that respects the dignity and decency of other persons. In his fine little book *Uncommon Decency*, Richard Mouw describes civility as "public politeness. It means that we display tact, moderation, refinement and good manners toward people who are different from us."[6] In other words, a civil person refuses the PC demand to hypocritically suppress our convictions. We keep our convictions because they are based in truth and relevant to the common good. Yet out of love for our neighbor and concern for our Christian witness, we express our convictions in a kind and thoughtful manner. To put it in biblical language, we combine what the apostle John said was true of Jesus' ministry—truth and grace (cf. John 1:14).

Civility is a lost virtue today. The people who are most passionate about an issue seem to think they *have* to be uncivil when expressing their views on it. In the mind of most people, politics is "nothing but war," which means, in their mind, that anything goes. If you're in a war, fight dirty. Lie about your opponent. Misrepresent him. Degrade him. Paint him as a thoroughly reprehensible person in whom nothing good can be found.

This approach is beneath us as citizens and especially as Christians. This sort of incivility is not only distasteful but sinful. As Christians, our lives must be characterized by conviction and civility.

Now, before we go any further, let me answer the objection that civility betrays weakness. This is almost too absurd to require a reply, but as I'm long-winded and already rolling, I'll indulge it.

If you want to be weak, just conform to the PC regime. Pretend to believe what you are told to believe. Act as you are told to act. Capitulate. Shoot, go ahead and buy into their hype. Shout down everyone who crosses the PC lines. But realize that as you do this, you're more like a toddler throwing a tantrum than the strong warrior you imagine yourself to be.

If you want to be strong, be civil. Show the strength that few possess—the power of self-control. Civility, in a phrase, is strength under control. It is the ability to resist our worst impulses, the capacity to honor people (1 Pet. 2:17) and live peaceably with them (Rom. 12:18) even when we find ourselves at odds. Anyone can fly into a rage. It takes true strength to be slow to anger.

What does civility look like? First, it necessitates a genuinely civil *approach to life*. It involves practicing empathy toward other people and being curious about their experiences and perspectives. It includes listening to our opponents' arguments not merely to counter them but also to understand. It means being genuinely open to correction, admitting the possibility that our current views are wrong. Biblical convictions aren't wrong, but our particular interpretations and applications of the Bible often are. It is a mark of strength, not weakness, to admit when we are wrong. I've heard it said that no one should ever be afraid to admit when they're wrong because it only proves they're wiser today than yesterday.

Second, it entails civil *speech*. These days the "American way" is to represent our opponents as stupid or bad or both. When engaging in public debate, we are not content to disagree with people but prefer to disparage them also. I've been guilty of succumbing to this temptation plenty of times over the course of my life, Christian. It is not easy to stand there in the moment and react civilly when another person is misrepresenting your views, unfairly questioning your motives, or stereotyping you.

Easy or not, we must be convictional and civil. Verbal incivility signals to the world that we are self-centered ideologues whose goal is to make ourselves look good or gain power at any cost. It also signals that we feel threatened by or afraid of our opponents' views; we don't think we can win a fair fight, so we have to play dirty. It says less about our beliefs and more about our character. But if we express our views fairly and out of genuine Christian love and concern, we signal to the world that Christians are both a strange people and a good people who want the best for our nation.

We Christians, after all, are the ones the apostle Paul instructed to be "speaking the truth in love" (Eph. 4:15). If we conform to the PC regime, we fail to be truthful or loving. But if we determine to be convictional and civil, we have the opportunity to display both truth and love.

So, let's resist the temptation to ignore either part of that command: the truth speaking or the genuine concern for the other person. If we speak the truth in love, and if that becomes a hallmark of Christian political activism, we can play a more significant role in making politics healthy again. Wouldn't that be something?

Yours,
Bruce

CHAPTER 13

BEWARE THE GIANT OCTOPUS

Christian,

Sure, we can tackle "big government" as our next topic. It needs tackling for sure, in more than one sense of the word. As I've mentioned before, government can swell to gigantic proportions, like a giant octopus reaching its tentacles into every social sector and cultural institution. It's an apt analogy; governments do tend to interfere in places where they have no business.

There are many examples of government reaching its tentacles into our social and cultural institutions—families, businesses, nonprofits, and so forth. But the most obvious example is the economy. Ronald Reagan once said, "Government's view of the economy could be summed up in a few short phrases: If it moves, tax it. If it keeps moving, regulate it. And if it stops moving, subsidize it." Well put, right?

Governments everywhere tend to expand their own jurisdictions until nothing is exempt from their micromanagement.

This isn't generally a plot on the part of specific people (though many people *do* intend to grow the government's size). It's simply that the inertia of government *as government* tends toward expansion. It's best to recognize this as one of the laws of nature rather than looking for specific villains. Rocks sink. Babies cry. Snakes bite. And governments expand.

Now just because we recognize this expansion as a fundamental law doesn't mean we quietly accept the consequences. We should be just as vigilant to stop the expansion of government as we are cautious to avoid snakebites. But the first step is calling a spade a spade. Or in this case, a snake a snake.

Not everyone agrees that big government causes society to wither rather than flourish, so I want to make that case here. But first, since I'm using the government-economics intersection to illustrate my point, let me take a moment to outline a biblical view of wealth and economics.

As I've mentioned before, the Bible teaches that God created a good world that would supply human needs and enable us to flourish. But in order for humans to flourish amid the riches of his creation, he wanted them to work. He told them to till the soil, bringing out the creation's hidden potentials (Gen. 1:26–31; 2:15). If they would do that, they would prosper. And prosper they did. They had an abundance of wealth but not even an ounce of the wealth-related sins we now experience—no envy, no greed, no theft.

All of that changed in the aftermath of the fall, as human beings began to sin. Suddenly wealth—and the possibility of greater wealth—became an occasion for sin. You can think of wealth-related sin in three broad categories.

First (and, in fact, at the heart of the fall itself), is the illicit *acquisition* of wealth. Adam and Eve insisted on acquiring the one thing God had forbidden them to acquire—fruit from the tree of knowledge (Gen. 3:1–6). Their sin was a sin of theft. As humans, all of us have inherited their sinful tendency to take what isn't ours. That's why the Bible repeatedly tells us not to covet (Exod. 20:17) or steal (Exod. 20:15) and to work hard and be content with what we receive (Prov. 30:7–9).

Second, we sin in our *use* of wealth. We pursue wealth for the wrong reasons (James 4:3) and use our wealth to benefit ourselves rather than others. In response to our illicit use of wealth, the Bible repeatedly urges us to be generous to others just as God has been generous to us (1 Tim. 6:17–19). After all, what we choose to do with our wealth reveals what type of person we truly are.

Last, but certainly not least, we sin by having a disproportionate *love* of wealth. Our human tendency is to love money and possessions with an ultimacy that should be reserved for God alone. When we elevate wealth to the status of lord and savior, we will do anything to acquire it, including breaking God's law and trampling other people. The irony is that wealth, while a good servant, is a harsh lord. When we allow it to rule over us, it leads to misery rather than happiness (1 Tim. 6:10). When we love it disproportionately, we can never get enough of it (Eccl. 5:10). And that is why the Bible repeatedly warns us not to make wealth into an idol (Matt. 6:19–24). A truly wealthy person is one who loves God rather than wealth (Luke 12:13–21).

The creative combinations in which we sin with our wealth are legion. Especially as it relates to poverty, even our "solutions" tend to be shot through with sin. When we see poverty, we ignore it. We refuse to be generous with our possessions. We misunderstand the holistic nature of poverty, how it affects a person at the core of his or her being.

We propose misguided solutions to poverty, solutions that might alleviate our guilt but harm those who are financially disadvantaged rather than helping them. (I think socialism does exactly this; it makes things worse instead of making them better.[1] But I am getting ahead of myself.)

The point is this. We should be grateful to God for creating a world of material abundance. We should work hard to earn wealth, use our wealth in wise and generous ways, and resist the disproportionate love of wealth that destroys our souls and divides our communities. At the same time we should mourn the existence of poverty and work hard to help those who are poor. We should help find sustainable ways for them to climb out of material poverty.

Now to turn our attention more directly to your initial question: the American government's proper relationship to its economy.

If we, as Christians, aim to work hard to acquire wealth, use our wealth in wise and generous ways, and are careful not to idolize wealth, is there a type of economic system that best facilitates our aim? I think so. It's a responsible free market or "small government" economy, one in which the persons in the political sphere do not intervene heavily or disproportionately in the economic sphere. A responsible free market is the best environment for job creation. It empowers individuals, communities, and institutions to help people climb out of poverty. And, unlike socialism or crony capitalism, it does not absolutize material equality or wealth.

Let me explain.

Renowned investor Ray Dalio helps us understand the market economy by describing it in terms of transactions:

An economy is simply the sum of the transactions that make it up. . . . A transaction consists of the buyer giving money (or credit) to a seller and the seller giving a good, a service or a financial asset to the buyer in exchange. A market consists of all the buyers and sellers making exchanges for the same things—e.g., the wheat market consists of different people making different transactions for different reasons over time. An economy consists of all of the transactions in all of its markets. So, while seemingly complex, an economy is really just a zillion simple things working together, which makes it look more complex than it really is.[2]

So a market consists of all the buyers and sellers making exchanges for the same things. The buyers and sellers can be individuals, families, nonprofits, partnerships, corporations, or even the government. Notice that each of these buyers and sellers in the market is an entity we'd say has its own "sphere of authority." What unifies them, economically speaking, is simply that they are exchanging goods. They are all giving and receiving *stuff* (that's a technical economic term).

A market such as this allows people to make decisions for themselves. For example, if I want to buy three racks of ribs and a bottle of John Boy and Billy's Grillin' Sauce, and the grocery store is willing to sell it to me, the government shouldn't have the authority (without a good reason) to say that I can only purchase two racks of ribs and no bottle of sauce. I should have the freedom to make this type of transaction because I am buying the food for my family (the familial sphere) and with my own money (the economic sphere). The government should not intrude.

One key reason the government shouldn't get in the way of my ribs is that I have information that is better and more relevant to my concerns than they do. In this case, I know how many people I'm feeding and their dinner preferences. In most economic transactions, something like this applies. The buyer chooses from available products and quantities because he is best situated to know what he needs. Buyers can (and often do) choose poorly, but as a general rule it is rare that someone outside the buyer knows his purchasing needs better than the buyer.

The cumulative effect of buyers making choices (three racks of ribs, not two) produces information about supply and demand that is collected and transmitted by the market. In other words, the market is not only a supply-and-demand system; it is also an information system. It creates, collects, filters, processes, and distributes information about people's economic preferences. The information in this particular system allows people to know whether and under what conditions they are willing to engage in the exchange. People on both sides of a transaction engage in it for their own benefit; if they did not expect to gain, they would not agree to the exchange.

A truly "free" market is one that functions as an information system (creating, collecting, filtering, processing, and distributing information) *largely free of distortions*. It allows buyers to tell the system what they want. More importantly, it allows them to tell the system how much they're willing to pay for it.

Imagine you purchase a bag of Sumatran coffee beans for $10.49. That single number—$10.49—represents the coming together of an unimaginable amount of information. The cost of the ingredients, of production, shipping to the store, etc., is all embedded in that $10.49. That price tells us—through a complex and multifaceted process—what people will likely pay for a bag of Sumatra coffee beans and what it took to get it to you.

So why do we sell bags of Sumatran coffee beans for $10.49 but sell Jeep Wranglers for $30,000? Who makes that decision? In a free market the decision is mostly made by the consumer. Not directly, of course, and not by the consumer alone. But as economist Don Boudreaux explains, "Prices reflect the value consumers think the products are worth. Whether it's the price of a bottle of ketchup or a Hermes Birkin purse, the price tag is the end result of a 'global chain of cooperation.'"[3]

But what if the government jumps into the middle of that chain? What happens if the government, intending to make goods and services more affordable, intervenes in the market? Often bad things.

Government intervention distorts the market and, by doing so, tends to hurt the very people it intended to help. No matter how well intended, the government can't possibly know as much about the market as the market knows about itself; as a result, government intervention causes unintended consequences we can never foresee. I'll let you guess whether these surprise consequences are generally better or worse than the government's initial expectations.

Philosopher and economic theorist Jay Wesley Richards often illustrates this point by telling the story of government experiments with rent control.[4] In the 1970s and 1980s, many city councils in the U.S. wanted to make housing prices more affordable for low-income renters—an obviously good intention. So they decided to cap what landlords could charge for rent. Nobody doubts that their motive was to help the poor. Ironically, however, their well-intended action had the worst possible consequence. Instead of expanding the affordable-housing options for the poor, it created a massive shortage in low-income housing.

To understand why, Richards says, think about these rent restrictions from the perspective of the landlords. They weren't necessarily greedy, but they did have to make enough money to stay in business. Imagine a landlord whose apartment building had twenty-five small apartments well suited to low-income renters. Each unit costs $1,000 to maintain, but city regulators have capped the rent at $500, so the landlord begins losing a significant amount of money. Given the situation, the landlord has a choice: either stop spending money to maintain the apartments (in which instance the property eventually becomes a slum) or convert the apartments into condos or commercial property (in which instance the property is no longer subject to rent control). The outcome is predictably tragic: eventually the options for the poor are fewer and lousier.

There are, of course, instances in which the government should intervene in the market to prevent exploitation. It should not allow jobs and wages to be forced on people who cannot consent (such as children) or to allow people to engage in work that is morally corrupting (such as the sex slave trade). In times of emergency—say, for instance, a hurricane—the government serves a helpful role by capping the price on certain necessary goods like gasoline and groceries. I'm sure you can think of some other instances.

But the government should be careful not to inhibit people's freedom to make morally worthy choices *simply because it disagrees with what they consider to be an acceptable gain from the exchange*. In almost every case free markets are the better option for free people.

Now I should point out that the U.S. economy isn't a perfect model of the free market. We've gone "off the rails" with several corruptions that sour the market. One of the worst corruptions of the free market is through "crony capitalism" or "corporatism."

In crony capitalism the government appoints regulators to control corporations. Often the regulators work in the offices of those corporations, causing the regulators to lose their objectivity and become, effectively, part of the corporation.

For government officials this scenario allows them to control the corporation without any personal risk. If things go well, the government gets the praise. If things go badly, the government gets the praise. Additionally, it allows the government to protect certain strategically important financial institutions. It gives to these institutions by subsidizing them and ensuring they will not fail. It takes from them by reaching its regulatory tentacles into their business. For corporations this scenario can be attractive because it allows them to collude with the government to undermine corporate competitors and protect the corporation. But the consumer doesn't usually fare as well.

So, a free market system can be—and always is, to some extent—corrupted because the people in that system are sinners. But it is better by far than a socialist system in which the government reaches its tentacles into the market, with negative and sometimes devastating consequences. Historically, socialist economies tend to foster a certain type of material equality—the type in which all ships sink equally with a receding tide. By contrast, however, a responsible free market fosters healthy competition between businesses, which in turn encourages businesses to offer better services and products. This sort of free-market model, to the extent it is inhabited by moral people, provides the ideal environment for society to flourish.

Speaking of flourishing, I hope you enjoy the trip home this weekend, especially the dinner with your extended family. Once you're back from the trip and ready to pick things up again, let me know.

Yours,
Bruce

CHAPTER 14

NO NEED FOR MULLAHS
AT 1 FIRST STREET

Christian,

It's good to hear from you again. I'm glad CCNN gave you a few days off to visit your parents. It sounds like you enjoyed catching up with the family but had a difficult time carrying on a civil discussion on political matters. Color me unsurprised.

I want to focus on the dinner conversation with your parents and your Uncle John, a man who grows more legendary with each letter you send me. You've mentioned your extended family a few times in your previous letters, but Uncle John always stands out. If he really is, as you mentioned, "farther to the Right than a tricycler on the Autobahn," and "more interested in venting his spleen than having a serious conversation," then I imagine he has equally dogmatic views about every topic he discusses, political or otherwise. (God help us if he's a college football fan.)

An "Uncle John" might be ignored in certain families, but he's considered a political genius in yours. His younger brother—your dad—may not be *as* inflammatory, but he seems to like John's verve. Of course, your dad can spit fire in his own right too. For instance, referring to people as "sissies" and "losers" when they call for civility in political discourse. An insult like that betrays a certain type of conservative mind-set that thinks it's justifiable to mock and demean those with whom we disagree on public matters.

I can understand why you quit the dinner table. I don't even blame you too much for telling them that it seemed unfair to continue in a battle of wits with such lightly armed men.

But you *do* need to extend a little more grace. It's particularly challenging with family, but if you can learn it there, you can apply it anywhere. The challenge before you is to find a way of respecting the people with whom you argue and of being tough enough to control your emotions in the middle of a debate. Your Uncle John may want to start a fight every time you meet. Resist. As my father often said, "Don't wrestle with a pig. You both get dirty, but the pig likes it."

You might want to consider finding some common ground with the person across the table (for example, your pro-life commitments) and only afterwards discuss issues on which you disagree (for example, Uncle John's white nationalism).

So let's talk about one of the issues where you probably have some common ground with your dad and maybe even Uncle John—the Supreme Court and constitutional interpretation. We'd planned to discuss constitutional interpretation anyway—why not move it up in the queue?

I know Dupont requires you to take a constitutional law course during your sophomore year, which is just a few weeks away now. That course is taught by a former clerk for Justice Ginsburg. Like Ginsburg, he takes a "living document" view of constitutional interpretation. Your dad wouldn't be pleased.

I agree with your dad, but I'll build my argument a little differently from him by giving some explicitly *Christian* reasons for rejecting your professor's view. But before we talk about that, I want to address the legal debate itself and some of the reasons your dad (most likely) and I reject the "living document" view.

As I see it, a number of Supreme Court justices have used their place on the bench to impose their moral views on American society. Instead of interpreting the law (the proper role of the judiciary in our country), they've arbitrated morality and have employed a "living document" view of the Constitution in order to do so. This imposition, no matter how well intended, undermines our democratic republic.

How does the "living document" view undermine our republic? I thought you'd never ask.

Most proponents of the "living document" view contend that the Constitution's framers specifically wrote the Constitution in broad and flexible terms so that future judges could reinterpret it in light of "the times." In effect, justices who employ this view from the Supreme Court bench are able to take things out of the Constitution that they do not like and insert things they do. Then they have the audacity to say the original writers would be cool with it!

When I think of the violence this does to the Constitution as a document, it puts me on the verge of hyperventilation. I like literature. And I respect it. So each time I encounter a text being manipulated by somebody who should know better, a little piece of me dies on the inside. I'd hate it if someone did that with my pleasure reading—say, *A Confederacy of Dunces* or *The Presidents Club*. How much worse when they do it to a text as crucial as the Constitution?

And yet, past Supreme Court Justices William Brennan, Thurgood Marshall, Earl Warren, and David Souter devoted their careers to doing just that—inventing novel meanings and violating the Constitution's integrity. Today, justices such as Ruth Bader Ginsburg and Anthony Kennedy do likewise.

Consider how the SCOTUS majority bypassed the text of the Constitution and historical tradition in order to create a right to privacy. This right to privacy (not in the Constitution, mind you) gave them the rationale to strike down state laws that restricted abortion in *Roe v. Wade* (1973). Or, consider the "right" to same-sex marriage that was created out of thin air in the 2015 *Obergefell v. Hodges* decision. Both of these decisions open the door for radical social transformation, and both of them arrive at their conclusions by taking inappropriate liberties in their interpretation of the Constitution.

Now hear me clearly: the Constitution isn't a perfect document. We've amended it several times in our history, and we may need to do so several times more. But dang it, *we have a process for changing it.* The process is intentionally cumbersome because our nation's founders didn't want the unelected lawyers of the SCOTUS to go about the business all by themselves. Amendments to the Constitution were meant to come by the vote of the people and only with an overwhelming majority in Congress and in the state legislatures. It's not an efficient way to change, but it's a democratic one.

Proponents of the "living document" view have managed to subvert the amendment process entirely, imposing social transformation on us by the decisions of a handful of begowned Ivy League lawyers. In effect, they are saying that We the People are either too ignorant or immoral to make decisions of this magnitude; we need activist courts to protect us from ourselves. As a general rule they don't say this explicitly. Usually they just imply it.

We the People shouldn't be so easily cowed. The justices of the Supreme Court have neither the qualifications nor the legal right to reign as philosopher kings.

That said, how should Americans respond to the situation?

We the People (and this is where you and your dad should find common cause) should demand an "original meaning" view of the Constitution, over and against the "living document" view. Supreme Court justices should interpret the Constitution in the way that people living at the time of its adoption would have. The Constitution means what it meant to the ones who ratified it in 1788; they are, after all, the authors, and the author has the authority. If we want to change it, which we very well might, then let's respect the process we have in place.

Each time the SCOTUS majority leans upon the "living document" view to make rulings that foster social transformation, it undermines us, the People. Consider Justice Scalia's rebuke of judicial activism in his dissenting opinion in the Obergefell case.

> Hubris is sometimes defined as o'erweening pride; and pride, we know, goeth before a fall. . . . With each decision of [the Supreme Court] that takes from the People a question properly left to them—with each decision that is unabashedly based not on law, but on the "reasoned judgment" of a bare majority of this Court—we [the People] move one step closer to being reminded of our [the People's] own impotence.[1]

Similarly: "To allow the policy question of same-sex marriage to be considered and resolved by a select, patrician, highly unrepresentative panel of nine is to violate a principle even more fundamental than no taxation without representation: no social transformation without representation."[2]

American citizens have a vested interest in electing a president who will nominate the type of Supreme Court justices who will respect the Constitution of the United States by reading it the way it was meant to be read. They deserve a SCOTUS who will respect its own role as a judiciary branch rather than bypassing Congress to legislate from the bench.

One more thing. I know many so-called conservatives who want to fill the Supreme Court bench with *their* people, using the same tactics to push a contrary agenda. I understand their motivation, and I completely agree that we should work to undo the damage the Supreme Court has wrought. But if what I'm saying here is true—that the Supreme Court *shouldn't* be a lever we can push and pull to get our own way—then we should practice the kind of integrity that refuses to use illegitimate power, even if given the chance. It may be expedient for us to act like an oligarchy when it suits us. But it can't last. And it's not worthy of our democratic republic.

Now, what, you ask, is a specifically *Christian* reason for adopting an "original meaning" view of constitutional interpretation?

The Bible has a lot to say about words and meaning. God's nature as Trinity means that meaning matters. God the Father is depicted as the one who speaks. God the Son is the Word spoken. God the Spirit is portrayed as the one who enables us to understand the Word that is spoken. This biblical pattern has always caused Christians to care about words and sentences and their meaning. Christianity, even when it wasn't intending to, has always produced a "bookish" people.

Now, of course, the primary way Christians have shown they care about words is through their devotion to the Bible. And the Constitution is not the Bible. We make no claims about its divine origin or about the inerrancy of its "doctrines."

But the Constitution is like the Bible in one key way: it is a foundational charter for a people. And just as Christians should respect the church's charter text, Americans should respect our nation's charter text. Just as Christians have experienced the havoc wreaked on Christianity when a "living document" approach is employed in biblical interpretation (don't get me started), so Americans will experience the havoc wreaked on our nation when a "living document" approach is employed in constitutional interpretation.[3]

I'll remind you that I'm not a legal scholar. My primary contention with the "living document" argument is one of literary integrity. I think I'm right, of course. But let me supplement my musings here with some reading from a legal giant.

Since you're busy with your CCNN internship, I suggest you begin by reading a short article that really packs a punch: the transcript of a speech given by Justice Scalia titled, "Mullahs of the West: Judges as Moral Arbiters."[4] Fetching title, eh? His point is that the Muslim office of mullah combines the tasks of legal interpretation and moral arbitration, but the American office of Supreme Court justice does not (well, *should* not) combine those tasks. The Constitution calls for Supreme Court justices to be interpreters of the law, but nowhere does it give them the right to be moral arbiters or social activists.

A final thought. I wonder how a liberal legal theorist would react if his readers employed a "living document" view of his opinion columns, reinterpreting his words to fit their preferences. Or how Justice Ginsberg would react if we assured her that her last will and testament would be interpreted as a "living document." Or, better yet, how one of Dupont's law professors would grade your exam if you purposely interpreted the exam's questions in a way differently than he intended. One imagines, in each instance, they would be indignant. And rightly so. As Americans, we must hold the SCOTUS to the same standard. We must say, "No constitutional adjudication without responsible interpretation."

So, Christian, you and your dad should be able to find some common ground on this one. (Savor it if you can because I'm sure you'll be at loggerheads again soon enough.) Americans have no need for mullahs at 1 First Street in Washington, D.C., the Supreme Court building. We should elect representatives who will nominate and confirm Supreme Court justices who will respect the Constitution by reading it the way it was meant to be read, who reject precedents that fail to meet this standard, and who view their role as interpreters of the law rather than as moral arbiters or social activists. Let's at least pretend we're running a democratic republic here.

That's all for now. I'm enjoying the conversation, and I'm encouraged to see you wrestle through the issues. Let me know when you're ready to march on to the next one.

Yours,

Bruce

CHAPTER 15

HITTING THE BULL'S-EYE
ON GUN LEGISLATION

Christian,

I'm happy to hear you were able to find some common ground with your family on the Supreme Court issue. And yes, I'm happy to discuss gun rights and gun control with you. In fact, we might kill two birds with one stone; in addition to helping you meet your deadline for the CCNN opinion piece about gun legislation, I might be able to persuade you that your father and your Uncle John are right to push back on some of your views on this issue.

Don't get too bent out of shape: it's not often that I get to take Uncle John's side, so let him have this one. If it helps, you don't have to tell him I've betrayed you.

I appreciate your desire to reduce violence in our nation and recognize that much of that violence comes down the barrel of a gun. But I want to challenge your assumption that our Christian commitment necessarily implies strict gun control legislation. There is no silver bullet for reducing violence in the U.S., and if there were one, it would not be gun control.

I know you are not "with me" yet. That's OK. I only ask that you consider what I have to say.

Let's start with our common ground. You and I both recognize that the issue of gun control is more complex than most people initially imagine. To arrive at a well-informed conclusion on these matters, we need a basic understanding of the legal and ethical dimensions of the debate. So let's discuss those dimensions before we begin to draw conclusions. Deal?

First, the legal debate. Like it or not, the U.S. Constitution is on your uncle's side. The Second Amendment to the Constitution states, *"A well regulated Militia, being necessary to the security of a free State, the right of the people to keep and bear Arms, shall not be infringed."*

Now, that statement might seem simple enough—it certainly is to Uncle John—but its interpretation is one of the most hotly disputed issues in our nation right now. The debate centers on whether the Second Amendment merely protects the *States'* rights to form militias (in order to hold the Federal government accountable) or if the right of gun ownership also extends to individuals (in order to keep weapons for self-defense).

Those persons who emphasize the first interpretation point to the 1939 Supreme Court ruling in the *U.S. v. Miller*. The *Miller* case determined that citizens should not be permitted to transport sawed-off shotguns across state lines. Why? Because short-barreled shotguns are not essential for military service in the states' militias. Short-barreled shotguns are nearly useless for a militia but obviously useful in warding off a home invasion. This interpretation served as the case law for subsequent lower court rulings over the next six decades.[1]

Persons who emphasize the second interpretation point to the 2008 Supreme Court ruling in *District of Columbia v. Heller.* In a 5–4 outcome, the justices struck down Washington, D.C.'s laws that banned handguns and required all long guns in houses to be stored disassembled and locked with a trigger lock. Justice Scalia's majority opinion reasoned that the District of Columbia violated citizens' rights by banning an entire class of firearms that are purchased most often for the express purpose of self-defense.[2] In other words, the ruling determined that American citizens have a constitutional right to keep and bear arms *outside of the context of a state militia*, even though the federal and state governments have a right to set boundaries on the type and proper use of weapons.

It seems to me that the second interpretation is the right one. Historically it's the interpretation most citizens and many scholars have held. Additionally, it's the most recent ruling, and it safeguards citizens' rights to own weapons.

Second, the ethical debate. Perhaps you'll allow that the Constitution protects gun ownership. But you think the Constitution is *wrong.* Fair enough. Let's assume the Constitution were not an obstacle. Should Christians push for gun control—and, if so, what *type* of control? This, Christian, is the question you're asking.

You laid out a well-intentioned and reasonable case in defense of your view. You cited some global studies that you think demonstrate the effectiveness of gun control in reducing gun violence. Based on those studies, you think heavier gun control would protect citizens from violence. Fewer guns means fewer people getting shot by guns, right? Additionally, you argue that, since Jesus is the exemplar for the Christian life, a Christian ethic based on Jesus' example should emphasize turning the other cheek. I'll admit it's difficult to imagine Jesus with a concealed sidearm.

In response, I'd argue that Scripture allows Christians to defend themselves, and weapons such as guns are acceptable instruments for self-defense. It certainly doesn't *necessitate* that Christians own weapons. I simply think pacifism is a misapplication of the ethics of Jesus. Jesus' "other cheek" analogy doesn't apply broadly to self-defense scenarios in a fallen world; instead, it urges Christians not to engage in vigilante justice, seeking revenge for wrongs done against them. Defending ourselves in the face of a violent attack is not vigilante justice. It is self-defense. Neither Jesus nor his apostles urged a position of strict pacifism. They discouraged *inappropriate* use of force while allowing *appropriate* use of force. As one plain example of this, when they interacted with soldiers, they *never* told the soldiers to simply put up their weapons.

As for the global studies you cited, they are not nearly as conclusive as you insist. Plus, there are empirical studies, such as Yale professor John Lott's *More Guns, Less Crime*, that draw the opposite conclusion. And there are nations, such as Switzerland, who have a high number of guns per capita but whose violent-crime rate is very low.[3]

Now, the legal and ethical rationales I've just provided have been expressed in only the briefest of forms. You probably won't be convinced on the spot. So I'll send a few articles and recommend a couple of books that go more in depth.

For now, at least provisionally, accept my train of thought and let's follow the rabbit trail. What kind of policy conclusions might my view lead to? If a Christian American could pull the trigger on passing gun legislation, what should he aim for? What would count as a bull's-eye? Although we don't have time or space to get into the finer points in the debate, I am comfortable unloading four principles from my mental magazine.

First, this issue is pro-life at its core. Any time we try to reduce violence against innocent persons—whether it is caused by guns or knives or embryotomy scissors—we are engaging in a pro-life project. The Bible teaches that all humans are created in the image of God, and it nowhere condones taking the life of innocent people. So when we realize that guns are sometimes used to take innocent lives and that some people want stricter gun control in order to reduce such violence, we should not be condescending or abrasive in our response to those people. People getting shot and killed is horrific and tragic. Our case for gun rights should do nothing to minimize this truth. Instead we should make the legal, ethical, and sociological case that in the United States innocent life is best safeguarded when citizens are able to own weapons.

Second, the Constitution does secure the right of citizens to own and carry guns. Although some constitutional scholars and historians argue that the Amendment was exclusively concerned with militia, *D.C. v. Heller* concludes that American citizens have the right to keep and bear arms outside the context of a state militia, within the context of federal and state regulations. This seems right.

Third, some minimal, constitutionally acceptable forms of gun control are wise. One example is legislation that prevents violent offenders and risky persons from legally obtaining guns. (The catch, of course, is how to define *risky*. Who is a risky person, and how can we keep a law such as this from being used as an instrument of oppression against "not risky but offensive and dissenting" voices in society?)

A positive example is the Terrorist Firearms Prevention Act (which did not receive the votes needed in the Senate to pass, though it did receive majority support). This Act called for the U.S. attorney general to block the sale of firearms to individuals on existing terrorist watch lists and called for the FBI to monitor gun sales through background checks, which would alert authorities on attempts to purchase guns if an individual had been on one of the government watch lists in the previous five years. This would have the effect of restricting firearms from being purchased by individuals who are currently under investigation and on a broader plane would alert local authorities to the purchase of guns by suspicious individuals without the need to ban sales to such individuals altogether.

What the bill would therefore accomplish is a greater *awareness* of gun sales without categorical *restriction* of those sales. Thus, it protects Second Amendment rights while also putting in place new regulations to address gun violence and domestic terrorism. I liked the Terrorist Firearms Prevention Act and wish the Senate had passed it.

Fourth, even if strict gun control were constitutionally acceptable, it likely would not reduce criminal violence in our nation. Violent offenders will find weapons, regardless of congressional legislation. Gun control would not have stopped Umar Farouk Abdulmutallab (the underwear bomber), Richard Reid (the shoe bomber), the Tsarnaev brothers (Boston bombers), or the September 11 hijackers (box-cutter killers). They all perpetrated (or attempted) their heinous violence with items that would be untouched by stricter gun regulations. Even if guns were completely illegal, the bad guys would have them. So why not let ordinary citizens have access to their own weapons?

Let me wrap up the letter by shooting straight with you for a moment: Christian, you need to do everything in your power to avoid the irrational fear of armed citizens (hoplophobia!) exhibited by most of your Dupont professors and peers. But you also need to steer clear of the neurotic obsession with firearms (hoplophilia!) exhibited on the Facebook pages of your high school friends—and yes, in the colorful life of your beloved Uncle John.

Speaking for myself, I want to keep people—especially my family—safe. I want to stop violent people from taking innocent lives. I'm willing to be convinced otherwise, but at this point in our nation's history, I think the best way to prevent violence against my family is by owning a gun. I'm peaceful by disposition, but I'm prepared in case a violent person comes against me or my family. Consider me a heavily armed dove, eh?

That's enough for now. I hope you continue to enjoy the summer. Let me know when you're ready to fire another volley my way.

Yours,

Bruce

CHAPTER 16

THE BEST EDUCATION FOR A TWENTY-FIRST-CENTURY AMERICAN

Christian,

I appreciated your response to my gun control letter. I can see that we agree on the basic principles but disagree a little bit in the application. Let me say clearly—that is OK. One thing American Christians must remember is that we do not have to agree on the minutiae of every single issue or policy matter.

What's our next target? By your prompting, it's education. I agree with you: many universities have lost their way. Instead of focusing their efforts on providing a rigorous and well-rounded education, they've poured their dollars and their energies into what Peter Augustine Lawler referred to as the "amenities arms race," a competition between colleges to see who can create the more luxurious hotel-style dorm rooms, gourmet food offerings, and state-of-the-art gyms. Maybe universities should put their cards on the table by marketing themselves straightforwardly as luxury resorts.

I could probably get over the pampering. More frustrating is the fact that many professors have shifted their goal from education to activism. Instead of making class a marketplace of ideas, they make it a hotbed of social action and, often, social outrage. Don't get me wrong; social action is good, but cultivating it is not the primary purpose of an educational institution.

But what gets under my skin the most may not be what you expect: college administrators are beginning to replace America's traditional model for education—liberal arts education—with a new competency-based model. In other words, they have stopped asking, "How can we best educate our students for their lifelong callings as citizens and workers?" and instead are asking, "How can we provide specific training so that our graduates can become immediately employed in a particular job?"

There is a helpful tension, of course, between getting a good (liberal arts) education and acquiring certain vocational competencies that help students get a job. Most students go to college for the stated purpose of helping their career prospects, so I'm not opposed to that motivation. Nonetheless, I think the strategy is counterproductive. A liberal-arts education instills some of the most important competencies students need to succeed in the real world, the ability to think critically, see the big picture, and so forth.

It's not just conservative professors like me who see things this way. Billionaire entrepreneur and *Shark Tank* celebrity Mark Cuban repeatedly emphasizes that a liberal-arts education is the best education for college students who will graduate and be forced to compete for jobs in a technology-savvy work environment. He argues that the liberal arts teach "soft skills" such as adaptability and communication that will give job seekers an advantage in the job market. He owns something like half of Texas, so I suppose we should listen.

Let's pause for a second and define our terms. What is a "liberal arts" education? When I talk about the "liberal arts," sometimes I receive puzzled inquiries: "I thought you were a *conservative*. Why would you recommend a *liberal* education?" I guess people asking this question hear "liberal arts" and assume I'm talking about Michael Moore films or something. But the liberal-arts education I'm talking about has nothing to do with America's political Left.

A liberal-arts education is "liberal" in the old sense of that word (you know how we professors like the "old senses" of words). By *liberal*, we mean wide-ranging, broad, and plentiful. The root word for *liberal*, *liber*, in Latin, means "free." A liberal-arts education frees us from the usual restraints that limit our learning. A liberal-arts education doesn't restrict our reading to books with which we already agree, books written in our day and time, or books about a specific vocation or workplace. Instead, it exposes us to many genres of literature written by many people over the course of many years. It counteracts our tendency to be provincial, to isolate ourselves from the past and from other perspectives. In other words, it provides an invaluable opportunity for us to transcend our limitations and achieve a well-rounded perspective on the whole of life.

A good liberal-arts education is often called a "classical education" because a broad and wide-ranging education involves reading classical literature—that is, works from the ancient, medieval, and modern periods. You know, *old stuff*. And instead of restricting a student's education to vocational reading (what will be immediately useful), it introduces them to the humanities (think literature, philosophy, music, art), the sciences (think biology, physics, sociology, psychology, and a whole host of other -ologies), and—in many instances—the disciplines of religious study. By exposing students to such a broad range of resources, a classical education helps them in ways that endure over the course of their lives, no matter what vocation or station of life they find themselves in.

Oh, wait. I can see it now. I can see the hands being raised in class every time I give this lecture on classical education. Maybe I should take the rest of my time here and answer a few questions. Yes? You with the green shirt, go ahead.

Q: *Professor Ashford, what can I do with a liberal-arts degree? How can the classics help me get a job?*

Well, the quick answer to that question is: a lot more than you can do with other, more "useful" degrees. By making you a well-rounded person who can adapt to a variety of workplaces, you position yourself to succeed in a number of different professional fields. Train yourself for one specific job, and you either (1) lock yourself into that for your entire life or (2) find yourself in a rough spot when the job market unexpectedly shifts—as happens more and more frequently in light of rapid technological change.

The reason a liberal-arts degree is so useful is because it teaches a student to think, communicate, imagine, and adapt to new environments and ideas. Mark Cuban put it well:

> I personally think there's going to be a greater demand in 10 years for liberal arts majors than there were for programming majors and maybe even engineering, because when the data is all being spit out for you, options are being spit out for you, you need a different perspective in order to have a different view of the data. And so [a person trained in the liberal arts will be] a freer thinker.[1]

Think about it. Most college freshmen don't know their abilities or options well enough to make an accurate or wise vocational decision. In fact, most college students change career plans *during* their four years of college, and they keep right on shifting after they graduate. Most college grads change jobs at least once within a few years of commencement. Fast-forward to ten years after graduation, and the likelihood that you're working the same job you planned to when you entered college *as a teenager* drops close to zero. (*Shark Tank* voice: "For these reasons, a 'useful' degree that focuses merely on competencies is actually quite useless, and, for that reason, I'm out.")

I see another hand over here on the left. Right here, with the ponytail. Yes?

Q: *Professor Ashford, you've described a liberal-arts education as one that includes study of the "classics." How can I tell a classic from all the other old books?*

In response to that question, Mark Twain once quipped that a classic is "a book that people praise and don't read." Funny and very true. Also sad because a classic is a text that has retained its value over the years. It has transcended its own moment in history. As the famous professor Northrop Frye wrote, a classic is "a work that refuses to go away."[2] It's got staying power.

What gives a classic such staying power? I have a short list to explain it. Humor me, if you will; list making is one of the core competencies of nerdy professors like myself.

1. A classic possesses excellence, both in content and form.

2. A classic has a universal appeal. That doesn't mean it lacks time-bound and local references. Rather, it deals with questions that appeal to readers from every era of history, a wide array of cultural backgrounds, and

a broad range of experiences. It challenges readers to seek truth, goodness, and beauty. It explores common themes such as life, death, love, hate, and faith. Even if the context is the Battle of Austerlitz in nineteenth-century Austria, you should be able to say, "I recognize this discussion, and it's one I need to hear."

3. A classic draws the reader into a broader conversation by making connections with writers and texts from other eras and disciplines.

4. A classic is influential. It shapes readers, writers, and often entire societies.

For these reasons, classics transcend the era in which they were written. In the words of philosopher David Hume, "The same Homer, who pleased at Athens and Rome two thousand years ago, is still admired at Paris and London. All the changes of climate, government, religion, and language have not been able to obscure his glory."[3]

Another question. You in the front. Have at it.

Q: *You've just described the qualities of the classics. But why should we read them?*

That is a very silly question, if in fact you did just listen to my description of a classic. Classics are deeply influential books that have had universal appeal over the centuries because of their ability to explore the most important themes in human life and answer the most significant questions humans raise. They're also often the most entertaining and enjoyable pieces of art that humanity has produced. Is that not enough to make you want to read them?

Granted, your college professors have some wisdom to pass along, and they may very well require you to read the best textbooks written *in the twenty-first century*. But I guarantee your college experience would be significantly enhanced if you were required to read the classics. They've been tried, tested, and proven worthy. Recent stuff? There's really no telling.

In the Old English epic *Beowulf*, the warriors prefer old swords to new ones because they consider them more effective and reliable. The same principle applies to books. We should prefer old books to new ones if we want to hone in on the profound questions of life and broaden our experience by transcending the fads and narrow views of our own era.

I see a hand way in the back, by the door. Go ahead.

Q: *I think you've convinced me. My problem is I'm not confident in my own ability to understand the classics. How should I go about reading them?*

That is a much better question than the last one. First, you need to make a plan to do at least a little bit of reading across a broad range of classics. You need at least a "coffee shop conversation" familiarity with all of the great books. For that purpose, you might begin by reading a one-volume collection of classic readings, such as Gamble's *The Great Tradition*. You might also read a book that summarizes and explains the classics; good examples are O'Hear's *Great Books* and Cowan and Guinness's *Invitation to the Classics*.

Second, you'll want to gain in-depth familiarity with at least a handful of the classics. For your money they're much better than the surveys anyway. If, for example, you want to become familiar with classics in politics, you could start by reading Plato's *Republic* and Aristotle's *Politics*, journey on to Augustine's *City of God*, take a deep dive into Machiavelli's *The Prince*, Hobbes's *Leviathan*, and Locke's *Second Treatise of Civil Government*, then finish the tour with Kant's *To Eternal Peace*, Mill's *On Liberty*, and Marx's *The Communist Manifesto*.

Third, you won't regret buying Adler and Van Doren's *How to Read a Book*, the updated edition of which not only provides a list of great books but also coaches the reader on how to read various genres—imaginative literature, stories, plays, poems, history, science, mathematics, philosophy, and social science—for all they're worth.[4]

For in-depth familiarity, read with a pencil in hand. Outline the book. Reread it. Wrestle with its ideas. Argue with the author in the margins. Don't look for "takeaways" and "action points" but for a mental experience that will prove enduring and enlightening.

As a Christian, you shouldn't hesitate to draw on the rich resources of Christianity as you analyze and evaluate these books. T. S. Eliot was right when he wrote,

> Literary criticism should be completed by criticism from a definite ethical and theological standpoint. . . . What I believe to be incumbent upon all Christians is the duty of maintaining consciously certain standards and criteria of criticism over and above those applied by the rest of the world; and that by these criteria and standards everything that we read must be tested.[5]

Last question. Go for it.

Q: *Sorry, mine is actually two questions. When you encourage us to read the classics, are you saying we should confine our reading to the bounds of Western culture? If so, what does Western culture have to say to blacks and other minorities?*

Good question, and my answer is twofold.

First, there's no good reason to confine yourself to the literature of Western culture. Since you live in the West, I think it is wise for you to focus your reading on the Western classics, seeking to understand the great debate that has unfolded over the centuries. Why wouldn't you want to gain a basic familiarity with Homer, Plato, Aristotle,

Virgil, Augustine, and Aquinas? Get to know Shakespeare, Descartes, Nietzsche, Hegel, and Freud, and you begin to understand both Western culture and life itself.

But it is also wise to read classics written in the global South and East. That's why, at my institution—The College at Southeastern—we require our students to read excerpts from the Bhagavad Gita, *The Analects of Confucius*, and the Qur'an, for example. Classics come from great minds, and great minds come from anywhere.

But, second, don't underestimate the ability of Western authors to speak to the concerns of minority communities. Western thinkers were the first to take diversity seriously and among the first to engage in serious criticism of ethnocentrism. I also point out that some Western classics, such as Shakespeare's *Othello*, explore the difficulties experienced by minorities seeking full citizenship in a majority-white context. Others, such as W. E. B. Dubois's *The Souls of Black Folk*, are written by black Americans to help black Americans understand themselves.

Speaking of understanding ourselves, I understand that once again I've written a stem-winder of a letter. I hope you have time to read it in the midst of your work at CCNN.

Yours,

Bruce

PS: I look forward to talking in person and meeting your family at the cookout this weekend.

CHAPTER 17

ONE MAN AND ONE WOMAN

Christian,

It was great to meet your family this weekend. I thought I was being invited to a laid-back cookout, but your Uncle John had different plans, eh? I should have expected it, considering your past descriptions of him, but there really isn't any replacement for the real thing. Guns, war, liberals, sex—saucy topics, indeed, for a family get-together.

I have to say, you handled yourself well, especially during the conversation about same-sex marriage. I'll say this for your uncle: when he makes a point, he makes it *emphatically.* Unfortunately, he also demeans and degrades every person with whom he disagrees, nephews not excepted. But you managed to keep your cool, setting the stage for a surprisingly civil discussion.

The historic Christian view of marriage is increasingly considered implausible and even harmful these days, even though it was probably the dominant view a generation ago. These days, it's become more popular to affirm same-sex marriage morally and politically, even in otherwise conservative circles. Those who oppose same-sex marriage are going against the grain, so they generally do so only under strong convictions.

The discussion this weekend started in the wrong place, as these discussions almost always do. Uncle John ambushed you with a question about the constitutionality of same-sex marriage, skipping completely over the more critical first things—God's design for marriage and sexuality and his desire for Christians to love and respect all people, including those with whom we disagree on matters of marriage and sexuality. Don't beat yourself up too much; the opportunity to have this conversation again is sure to come soon enough.

In your email this morning, you mentioned that you're new to Christianity and that you weren't sure how to articulate a biblical view of marriage and sexuality. You shouldn't feel so bad. There are Christians who are *not* new to the faith who can't articulate a biblical view of these important topics. Let me try to give a brief flyover of the biblical picture.

Marriage and sexuality make their appearance in the first chapters of the Bible. In the beginning God created humanity, "male and female," revealing that gender differentiation is part of creation's basic order (Gen. 1:27). The creation story culminates with God's instruction for the first man and woman to marry one another (Gen. 2:23–24) and to "be fruitful, multiply, fill the earth" (Gen. 1:28). As this passage reveals, and later biblical passages confirm, God designed marriage as an institution involving one man and one woman, with the potential for childbearing. The possible variations away from this creational ideal are rather complicated; the ideal itself is rather simple.

In the New Testament the apostle Paul builds on the creation account to argue that a man should love his wife sacrificially and wholeheartedly (Eph. 5:28–31) and that married couples should realize their marriage is meant to serve as a reflection of God's love for sinners. In other words, marriage should be a picture of the gospel (Eph. 5:32). When a Christian couple loves each other patiently and sacrificially over the course of a lifetime, their marriage reflects God's patient and sacrificial love for humanity. Paul's teaching on marriage doesn't overturn anything from the Genesis account, but it does heighten the (already) sacred basis of marriage.

What about the act of sex? Contrary to popular belief, the Bible is very pro-sex. It teaches that God created sex for us to enjoy within the bounds of marriage. But that last phrase, "within the bounds of marriage," has been a public point of contention in the United States for many years. More than a half century ago, many Americans began arguing publicly that sex outside of marriage is acceptable and good and even better than sex inside of marriage. Today the church has largely lost that argument. Societally speaking, it is a nearly incontrovertible truth that marriage isn't necessary for sex. We're all sexual creatures, so the assumption goes, and we have every right to satisfy that urge, whether married or not. Say that a person can be fulfilled without having sex, or that waiting until marriage to have sex is healthy, and you won't meet counterarguments. You'll be met with eye rolls and shrugged off as a naïve prude.

Most recently, the public points of contention have been homosexual sex and marriage. What does the Bible say about homosexual intercourse? It doesn't mention homosexual sex often, but when it does, it categorically prohibits it (Rom. 1:24–27; 1 Tim. 1:9–11). Considering the creational design, this shouldn't be an enormous surprise. But this aspect of Christian moral law shocks and offends many Americans today. It seems just as obvious that men can sleep with men as that men and women should be free to have sex outside of marriage. If it's mutual and it's fun, what's the big deal?

You shouldn't need a Bible to understand that men and women are biologically designed for heterosexual intercourse leading to childbirth (unlike same-sex intercourse). And history overwhelmingly favors the understanding of marriage as male-female. As ethicist Scott Rae notes, "No civilization has ever survived the destruction of the traditional family."[1]

That said, your Uncle John's rationale for heterosexuality was ham-fisted, and his comments about gay people were demeaning. He's a man, it seems, in whom the milk of human kindness has curdled. In opposition to his approach, Scripture calls us to recognize that all human beings have warped sexual desires. All of us are, in one way or another, broken, twisted, or bent. So, when we articulate a biblical view of marriage and sexuality, we should do so with humility, recognizing our own sin. And we should do so with love for our same-sex-attracted neighbor, who is broken in his or her own way.

The question remains: How should American Christians apply the Bible's teaching about marriage and sexuality to the twenty-first-century debate about the legality of same-sex marriage?

Let me start by saying that Christians shouldn't always want biblical teaching to be enshrined as the law of the land. In fact, there are many biblical teachings that I would actively work to prevent being made into law. Consider the Bible's command for every person to look to Jesus for salvation. There is no biblical teaching more important than that one. Yet, if that biblical teaching were made into a law, it would be forcing people to "love" Christ and live as if they were Christians. But forced love is rape, and forcing non-Christians to live as Christians would undermine the gospel and cause non-Christians to live as hypocrites. We've seen this kind of religious compulsion in the past, and the results aren't pretty.

That said, we shouldn't run too far the other way and conclude that "legislating morality" is a categorically bad decision. For one, many laws are moral. They identify certain behaviors as allowable and others as forbidden, and in so doing, they classify the forbidden ones as wrong. Christians, then, shouldn't be shy about sometimes wanting biblical morality to be enshrined into law. We should want the government to enforce laws against murder, theft, rape, and libel. We should want it to enforce laws that secure the church's right to preach the gospel, the family's right to raise and educate their own children, and so forth.

And yes, we should want the government to recognize that a "marriage" is a union between one man and one woman.

Now, don't get me wrong. I don't think we should make homosexual sex or homosexual relationships illegal, any more than I think we should make cohabitation illegal. Though some people disagree with me on this, I don't think outlawing the behavior is necessary. I would even go a step further and say that we ought to speak up for homosexual people whenever they are harmed, insulted, or slighted.

What I am saying is that it is dangerous to call a homosexual relationship a "marriage," no matter how loving, how long-term, or how monogamous it intends to be. Those qualities, while commendable, do not define a marriage. A marriage is a relationship between one man and one woman, with the potential for childbirth. This view is supported by humanity's biological design, most civilizations and world religions, and—most importantly—clear biblical teaching.

To call a committed homosexual relationship a "marriage" is to commit a category mistake, assigning to that relationship a quality or action which can only properly be assigned to things of another category.[2]

To this some might respond, "Well, so what if we change the category? What's so dangerous about tweaking a definition a little?" Category mistakes may not be a big deal if the categories are irrelevant or trivial and the scope is small. If my neighbor keeps calling his dog a "fur baby," I might find it annoying, but he's not trying to get dogs the same rights as children, so I just ignore it. But category errors become a big deal when the scope expands and they are backed up by force of law.

This is exactly what happened when in June 2015 the Supreme Court issued its ruling on the case of *Obergefell v. Hodges*.[3] In this landmark case the Court was asked to adjudicate a legal debate centering on two questions: (1) Does the Fourteenth Amendment require a state to license a marriage between two people of the same sex? (2) Does the Fourteenth Amendment require a state to recognize a marriage between two people of the same sex when their marriage was lawfully licensed and performed out of state? These are known as the "marriage" and "recognition" questions, respectively, and the Court answered both in the affirmative. Same-sex marriage is now a fundamental right.

On behalf of the majority, Justice Kennedy wrote, "The right to marry is a fundamental right inherent in the liberty of the person, and under the Due Process and Equal Protection Clauses of the Fourteenth Amendment couples of the same-sex may not be deprived of that right and that liberty. Same-sex couples may exercise the fundamental right to marry."[4]

The Court's ruling notes that marriage is already considered a "fundamental right" by the Supreme Court (correct) and thus must clearly apply to opposite-sex couples (not correct). In other words, they committed a category mistake. They called the same-sex relationship a marriage, declared it equivalent to man-woman marriage, and then codified it into law by defining it as a "fundamental right." They did nothing to demonstrate that this type of relationship was, in fact, a marriage. That step in the argument was assumed. But it's a pretty important step to skip.

Marriage is important, and part of that importance lies in knowing what the essence of marriage *is*. The court assumed, without proving, that monogamous love is the essence of marriage. This is a huge switch—one which the court had no authority to make. As Chief Justice Roberts wrote in his dissenting opinion, "[T]his Court is not a legislature. Whether same-sex marriage is a good idea should be of no concern to us. Under the Constitution, judges have power to say what the law is, not what it should be." Roberts added, "The majority's decision is an act of will, not legal judgment. The right it announces has no basis in the Constitution or this Court's precedent."[5]

The late Justice Antonin Scalia dissented also, writing, "Today's decree says that my Ruler, and the Ruler of 320 million Americans coast-to-coast, is a majority of the nine lawyers on the Supreme Court." He went on to assert that the Obergefell ruling "is a naked judicial claim to legislative—indeed, super-legislative—power; a claim fundamentally at odds with our system of government," and "a system of government that makes the People subordinate to a committee of nine unelected lawyers does not deserve to be called a democracy."[6] As you can tell, Scalia's beef was just as much (probably more) about the Court's subverting its role than about a particular sexual ethic. Judicial activism, which we've already discussed at length, simply isn't the way to make social, cultural, and political transformations of this magnitude.

Concerning judicial activism, the late Richard John Neuhaus once wrote, "Such judges belong to the New Class whose members select, reinforce, and reward one another on the assumption that they know better than ordinary people how we ought to live. They have few compunctions about making up law in order to coerce others into conforming with their understanding of virtue."[7] And, as we've seen the past few years, the Court's activism has undermined religious liberty, exacerbated our society's social and political polarization, and flung the door wide open for the Court to engage in social transformation projects that should be left to "We the People." Like Scalia, I'm not only concerned about the rise of an aberrant view of marriage; I'm also concerned about the subversion of our democratic republic. Both are poisons that will leave our society sicker.

A friend of mine often points out that the sexual revolution promises joy and fulfillment, but it can never keep those promises. The more the law of our land codifies the "freedom" of the sexual revolution, the more it will create people who are disappointed, wounded, and in worse bondage than before. Our role, as Christians, is to receive the "refugees of the sexual revolution" and to offer them something more permanent and true.[8]

That's our role as a church. Politically the question of same-sex marriage is a little more complex and multifaceted. But it can never involve less than our speaking the truth. We've all got to answer serious questions about constitutional interpretation and the place of the judiciary branch and serious questions about how best to give gay Americans the justice and equality they deserve *without* making the category mistake of describing a homosexual union as a marriage. For Christians it entails several other questions: What does the Bible have to say about marriage and sex? What is the appropriate relationship of biblical morality to twenty-first-century American civil law? How can I love my gay neighbor even when he or she may disagree with me about the nature of marriage?

I know CCNN might ask you to write an opinion piece on this topic whenever it next appears in the news cycle. I encourage you to begin thinking about it now. Maybe even write a blog series on the topic, being careful to interact seriously with the feedback you receive. Regardless, I'm encouraged by your willingness to be faithful even when you find yourself on the wrong side of history. And remember, Christianity is only on the wrong side of history if by *history* we mean current trends. But if history includes Christ's return to set the world aright, I guarantee you're not on the wrong side.

Yours,

Bruce

CHAPTER 18

TO SHAVE A YAK

Christian,

Nice work on the blog post you wrote about *Obergefell*. I've said it before, and I'll say it again: in our polarized political environment, a good opinion writer often will take incoming fire from both sides of a political dispute. As C. S. Lewis put it, "If the Patagonians think me a dwarf and the Pygmies a giant, perhaps my stature is in fact fairly unremarkable."[1] On this particular issue many of the Left-leaning comments accused you of being a hateful, bigoted, backwards, knuckle-dragging Neanderthal. Not surprising—many Americans equate disagreement with hatred. To your credit, at the same time folks on the Right came after you, calling you soft because you refrained from demeaning or mocking people who are same-sex attracted. Not surprising—many Americans think disagreement and degrading language should go hand in hand.

Speaking of disagreement and degrading language, our next topic for discussion—environmental ethics—is the one of the most divisive. It's divisive because it's important, and one of the reasons it's important is that debates about climate change, for instance, can help bring to the surface divergent views about the value of the natural world and of humanity's place in it.

Let me begin by summarizing four big-picture approaches to environmental ethics. To keep you from suspense, I think the fourth is the best path forward. Then I'll provide a few thoughts on what public policy might look like in light of a biblical perspective.

The first big picture approach to environmental ethics is *biocentrism*. Biocentrists contend that all living things have inherent worth. Many biocentrists also argue that all living things have *equal* worth. Thus humans are not more morally valuable than plants or animals.

The second big picture approach is *ecocentrism*. Ecocentrists argue that the ecosystem as a whole is worth more than its component parts, that the component parts include both living and nonliving things, and that human individuals are relatively unimportant in the scheme of things.[2]

The third approach is what I call *anthropocentrism*. Anthropocentrists argue that humans are much more important than other living or nonliving things. An anthropocentrist would see no problem with exploiting natural resources for human use because it's people that matter. The only time exploitative anthropocentrists might be concerned to *protect* the environment is if that protection will help future generations exploit it.

There's an element of familiarity in each of these three approaches, but they're all out of balance. Yes, biocentrists, all living things do have worth. Yes, ecocentrists, humanity should think of itself a bit more humbly. Yes, anthropocentrists, people are more valuable than rocks. But the better position isn't merely a combination of these three approaches. It's uniquely *theocentric*, which means five things:

1. God is the Creator and King of all things. As the psalmist says, "The earth and everything in it, the world and its inhabitants, belong to the LORD" (Ps. 24:1). We do not own the environment. In fact, we do not own a single blade of grass or the tiniest of animals. Everything on earth—including the earth itself—belongs to God (Job 41:11). Therefore, we must place him at the center of our environmental ethic.

2. God created everything that exists. Therefore, every aspect of God's creation has some type of inherent worth and dignity.

3. God created man and woman in his image, ascribing a unique worth and dignity to us. Therefore, God does value us in a more significant way than, say, ferrets (although a ferret does have its own worth).

4. Within a theocentric approach, there is, therefore, a hierarchy of worth and dignity. The entire created world is valuable, while human beings have a special value, and God—as the Creator and King—has the most value of all.

5. God created man and woman to be caretakers of his good creation (Gen. 1:26–31; 2:15). He gives us real authority by entrusting us with the task of cultivating the earth, not in an exploitative way but in a way that *both* respects its value and enables human beings to live and flourish.

The balance in that last point is the real challenge for us Christians. God calls us to be responsible stewards— *of* creation and *for* humanity—but it's not always easy to know when we've gone beyond "stewarding" and started "exploiting." Often it appears that there is a zero-sum game between humanity and the rest of creation: what is good for one is bad for the other, and vice versa. What then?

Consider, for instance, the most divisive debate in environmental ethics today—climate change. Is the globe warming? If so, is this climate change *cyclical* (something that happens globally every few centuries or millennia) or *human caused* (something that would not happen if humans hadn't polluted the globe)?

On the one hand, most scientists believe in climate change and think humans are causing it. On the other hand, many scientists (yes, real ones) do not. You'll find a similar split among us average nonscientists too. The arguments among the scientists vary. Some of them question the accuracy of climate-change projections. Others acknowledge climate change but view it as cyclical and attributable to natural causes. Still others acknowledge climate change but argue that we cannot know its causes.

But most of these arguments are happening between people like you and me. I'm not a scientist; I'm just a professor who teaches courses on Christianity, politics, and public life. And the Bible doesn't address the question of whether humans could or would cause global warming. Thus, the debate about climate change is outside of my sphere of expertise. I'll assume that either view is a legitimate possibility. We might or might not be experiencing human-caused climate change. So let's address this issue as a matter of practical politics. Let's ask what our political options are and then try to pick the one we think best.

One of my friends, Joe Carter, argues that there are only five real options and that those options can be derived from a combination of these three categories. This may get a little serpentine for a moment, but I think in the end this actually makes the situation clearer. Here are Joe's categories and options, with a few modifications:[3]

Category A (choose one)

1. The earth's climate is being significantly affected by human activities.
2. The earth's climate is not being significantly affected by human activities.

Category B (choose one)

1. The long-term effects will be catastrophic.
2. The long-term effects will not be significant.

Category C (choose one)

1. There is nothing we (can/need to) do about it.
2. We can avert disaster if we act now.
3. We may be able to avert disaster if we act at a future time.

These options can be combined in twelve possible variations, not unlike a Choose Your Own Adventure novel. But seven of them are logically absurd, so only five remain, which can be labeled as:

1. Do-Nothing Pessimism (1, 1, 1)
2. Act-Now Optimism (1, 1, 2)
3. Act-Later Realism (1, 1, 3)
4. Do-Nothing Optimism (1, 2, 1)
5. Skeptical Optimism (2, 2, 1)

Let's start at the bottom with Skeptical Optimism. Anyone who denies human climate change falls into this category. The skeptical optimist position is simple: humans aren't causing climate change and, for that reason, we cannot and should not try to do anything about it. I suggest we reject this view for two reasons. First, if the skeptical optimists are wrong, we're harming ourselves by not acting. That's an enormous risk. Second, this option is not viable politically at the moment. Even if this turns out to be the correct view (scientifically) of climate change, we might lose a lot of (political) capital by expending our energies fighting policies meant to counteract climate change.

Now let's consider the other do-nothing options—1 and 4. They come to the same conclusion ("no need to act") but for different reasons. In option 1, the do-nothing pessimist thinks humans are causing climate change *and* that the long-term effects will be catastrophic. But he thinks it's too late for us to do anything about it. The ship is sinking, and there's nothing we can do about it. In option 4, the do-nothing optimist thinks humans are affecting climate change, but climate change won't have significant long-term effects. Whatever we're doing to the environment isn't worth addressing. So we shouldn't. I don't like either of these views because they are too pessimistic and too optimistic, respectively. I'm a realist who rarely finds himself plagued by eternal pessimism or sunny optimism.

What about Act-Now Optimism? Act-now optimists are confident humans are causing climate change that is potentially catastrophic, but they're also confident that we can avert disaster if we act now. The downsides of acting now include: (a) if the act-now optimist is wrong to think climate change is caused by human activity or if he is wrong in his prescriptions, the regulatory policies he is pushing have serious economic downsides that hinder human flourishing; and (b) even if we could agree on what action would be most effective (a mammoth *if*), the most significant nations, China and India, would almost certainly refuse to make the same changes, rendering our climate-change-related regulations negligible.

We are left with Act-Later Realism. By process of elimination, that's where I land. I think this position dovetails nicely with the biblical position I described above, in which we actively seek to steward the earth's resources for human flourishing and do so in a way that doesn't intentionally exploit God's creatures. As to the specific question of climate change and its causes, I'm betting on future developments to bring clarity to the debate. Scientists may achieve a consensus about climate change and its causes. If they conclude that humans are causing global warming, I'm hopeful that we—and it would have to be a *global we*—could find and implement some technological solutions.

Now, Christian, just because the best solutions lie in the future doesn't mean act-later realists should do *nothing* now. We should be doing lots of things; it's just that those things will look more like "yak shaving" than addressing global warming per se.

To which you ask, "What in the world is 'yak shaving'?"

The term, oddly enough, originated in an episode of the 1990's era cartoon *Ren & Stimpy*. And in what has to be one of the stranger connections between "art" and science, it was later adopted by the MIT Artificial Intelligence Lab. Seriously. As Jeremy H. Brown explains: "[Y]ak shaving is what you are doing when you're doing some . . . fiddly little task that bears no obvious relationship to what you're supposed to be working on, but yet a chain of twelve causal relations links what you're doing to the original meta-task."[4]

"Yak shaving" sounds silly, but it's a smart practice. By taking many actions aimed at solving smaller problems, you may inadvertently solve or alleviate the larger problem that originally needed a solution.

Consider, for example, the claim that global warming will lead to an increase in the frequency and severity of hurricanes.[5] If this claim is true, we should expect to face future disasters on the scale of 2005's Hurricane Katrina. But while we may not be able to solve the global-warming problem, we *can* work on a seemingly unrelated problem that made Katrina especially deadly: poverty. As Joe Carter explains:

> Because authorities were unable to evacuate the city in a timely manner, Katrina had a disproportionate impact on the poverty-stricken residents of New Orleans. Many people died needlessly because they lacked even the basic financial means to escape the area. Alleviating poverty would not have prevented the hurricane from hitting Louisiana, but it could have lessened the impact and the loss of life. Similarly, reducing poverty will not prevent global warming from increasing the number or severity of future hurricanes. It would, however, make it considerably easier to live with such natural disasters.[6]

What I'm trying to say boils down to this: while the scientists duke it out with each other (and, unfortunately, with the politicians), one thing you and I, and other everyday Americans, can do is serve our nation selflessly. We can serve it in actionable and demonstrably effective ways, like disaster relief and poverty alleviation. We can focus our attention and resources on problems we know how to solve. And we can make small but significant adjustments to our lives, such as reusing and recycling, making responsible decisions about the types of automobiles we drive, and so forth.

This option won't be popular with many Americans. There's nothing particularly sexy about it. It lends itself to backbreaking and wallet-thinning service rather than to self-righteous political posturing and headline-making protests. But would you rather make the news or make a difference?

Act-Later Realism won't be popular with ecocentrists or geocentrists because it prioritizes action on behalf of humans. It won't be popular with anthropocentrists because it refuses to justify exploitation. So you might find yourself out there hanging in the wind, as they say, taking this approach all by your lonesome. But that's OK. You'll be loving your neighbor by working on relatively solvable problems as you wait for scientific consensus to help us get beyond the current impasse.

Keep your yak razor sharp, and I'll talk with you soon.

Yours,

Bruce

CHAPTER 19

WHAT HATH JUSTICE TO
DO WITH MERCY?

Christian,

It's good to hear from you again. Sounds like you had a great grill-out with your new friends from CCNN. (I can respect your "perfect" steak, seasoned with olive oil, kosher salt, and cracked pepper, cooked at 500 degrees for two and a half minutes on each side, but I'd be remiss not to say that the *perfect* steak is, in fact, marinated for several hours in a mixture of teriyaki and Italian dressing, then grilled at exactly 600 degrees for three minutes on each side. But I digress.)

Enjoy the summer because it will soon be over. Speaking of which, we've made a lot of headway on the public policy topics you wanted to discuss this summer. Only a small handful of topics are left to discuss. Why not talk about immigration next? As you mentioned in your letter, the specter of immigration reform sure does get people whipped up in a French-Canadian frenzy these days.

In fact, an old friend of mine unfriended me on Facebook because of my views on immigration reform. I might not have noticed—Facebook is discreet like that—except that before he pulled the plug, he fire-hosed me with angry comments, written with a furious use of all capitals and exclamation marks, and replete with insults. I mean, if he hadn't unfriended me, I might have had to break into his house and steal the "caps lock" and "!" keys from his laptop. My guess is that the absence of those two keys would have rendered him incapable of communication.

Facebook friends aside, immigration questions have been making the front-page headlines often of late. Recently, thousands of college students walked out of class to demand that their institutions declare themselves "sanctuaries" for undocumented immigrants.[1] Our last presidential election was swayed by the candidates' disparate stances on immigration reform. The executive and judicial branches of our government keep locking horns over it.

Even though the disputes over immigration came to a head during the 2016 election cycle, President Obama's administration clearly thought illegal immigration was a problem. Did you know he expelled more than 2.7 million unauthorized immigrants during his first seven years in office? In fact, President Obama's deportation policies earned him the title of "deporter-in-chief" from Clarissa Martinez de Castro of the Hispanic advocacy group National Council of La Raza.[2]

Regardless of who holds the office of president, questions about illegal immigration and immigration reform will probably not subside any time soon. Nor should they. This is an important debate for our nation to have. I hope we come down on the right side.

As I see it, Christian, our response to illegal immigration should be shaped by wisdom in holding together twin biblical virtues: justice and mercy. The Bible teaches that God ordains government in order to secure *justice* for the individuals and communities under its jurisdiction. Government secures justice, in part, by making and enforcing laws—including immigration laws. Every nation has a duty to serve its citizens by making immigration laws, outlining fair and clear immigration procedures. Every nation has a duty to serve its citizens by securing its borders and enforcing its laws by penalizing those who break them. These realities speak to the need for justice in immigration reform.

At the same time, the Bible repeatedly emphasizes that Christians should exhibit *mercy*. While our government and our nation should enforce its immigration laws, we should demand that it does so in a humane and compassionate manner. *Justice* need not mean "harshness."

Compassion seems sorely lacking from some quarters in our nation. It seems like many of our fellow citizens view immigrants as subhuman, as if they were animals or machines. I despise it when immigrants are stereotyped as if all of them are rapists or murderers (the animal analogy) or as if the only thing they're good for is lawn care or farm labor (the machine analogy). Immigrants are neither animals nor machines; they are human beings created in God's image (Gen. 1:26–27) and are the recipients of Jesus' love (John 3:16). For that reason the Bible makes clear that we should not oppress immigrants (Mal. 3:5) or treat them in ways that we would not want to be treated ourselves (Matt. 7:12).

After all, Christians believe Jesus will return one day to rule over a kingdom that includes worshippers from every tribe, tongue, people, and nation (Rev. 5:9). We must remember that many immigrants will one day be—and in Christ already are—citizens with us in the city of God. We share more in common with the Christian undocumented citizen who speaks no English than we do our documented American-born neighbor who is not a Christian.

Simply speaking of justice and mercy, however, doesn't automatically translate into public policy. How can we balance the two? I think the answer is twofold: our nation should (1) secure our borders immediately and (2) begin reforming our immigration laws and procedures in ways that are both just and merciful. Right now we aren't doing either very well.

As for secure borders, our nation has spoken out of both sides of its mouth for years. We've passed laws that make it illegal for immigrants to cross the border without gaining certain legal permissions and documents. Fair enough. But we haven't enforced those laws in anything resembling a consistent manner. It's as if we've said to the world, "Now, we've put some immigration laws on the books, but (wink, wink, giggle, giggle) we didn't really mean it. Feel free to ignore the law!" This doesn't even work with our toddlers, so I'm not sure why we think it'll work in international politics. Why should we crack down on people to whom we've sent such mixed signals? Shouldn't we first crack down on ourselves for undermining our own rule of law?

More important, we need to craft a new immigration policy that is consistently *just* (in recognizing that undocumented immigrants have broken a law) and *merciful* (in recommending a penalty that is humane and appropriate). Both justice and mercy are central to the Christian faith, and they should likewise be central to our treatment of persons who entered our country illegally.

To drill down to an even more specific level, I think our immigration reform should be characterized by at least seven nonnegotiables:

1. *A path to deportation.* We should agree to deport undocumented immigrants who have a criminal record in their nation of origin or in the United States.
2. *Multiple paths to legal status.* We should provide paths that allow undocumented immigrants to become citizens, to work in our nation for a limited period of time before returning to their country, or to work indefinitely while retaining citizenship in their home country.
3. *Incentives for selected immigrants.* We should provide incentives for highly skilled immigrants in order to bolster our nation's long-term economic competitiveness.
4. *Up-front limits on chain migration.* We should limit the influx of extended family members.
5. *Appropriate penalties.* We should not simply grant amnesty to those who have broken the law. If undocumented immigrants wish to gain legal status, we should allow it, but it's unjust to place them ahead of those who are already pursuing the process legally. Placing undocumented citizens "at the back of the line" to undergo a criminal background check and to pay some back taxes for previously undocumented income seems like a reasonable and humane punishment. Going to "the back of the line" doesn't mean they would be deported, but it does mean they would receive only provisional documentation while they wait in line to receive their green card or citizenship.
6. *Cutoff date.* We should provide a cut-off date to apply for legal status so that undocumented immigrants will come forward in a timely manner.
7. *Employer penalties.* We should build a responsive system that enables employers to verify an employee's

legal status quickly, and we should penalize businesses—appropriately and not cripplingly—for ignoring the legal status of their employees.

There's still a huge amount of room within that framework to figure out finer details. But if we could agree to those reforms, we'd be well on our way to speaking and acting with a more unified, just, and merciful voice.

One even more specific situation is worth mentioning—the Dreamers. Dreamers are minors who did not choose to come to the United States but who live here now because they were brought here by their parents. Their situation is unique, and I think it deserves special treatment.

My friend Alan Cross introduced me to the story of a Dreamer named Erick. Erick's parents brought him from Mexico to the United States when he was only two years old. He grew up in America and didn't even know he was an undocumented immigrant until he was a teenager. He has no memory of Mexico, speaks perfect English, and graduated from a California college with a degree in biochemistry. He is now in his midtwenties and has benefitted from the 2012 Deferred Action for Childhood Arrivals (DACA) policy, which allowed him to finish college. Alan met Erick and tells me he was amazed by Erick's determination and desire to contribute to America, the only country he knows. Erick intends to pursue a PhD and work as a researcher in the pharmaceutical industry.

But all of that is in jeopardy now. As I write this letter, our president has just repealed DACA. Many states have officially protested this repeal, and it is unclear, legally, what will happen to DACA. More critically, it is unclear what will happen to the 800,000 Dreamers, like Erick, whose future is now uncertain.

Alan and I have publicly encouraged American Christians to lobby for the protection of Erick and other Dreamers, even as we secure our borders and begin to enforce our immigration laws. The two aren't at odds.

Why should we advocate for Dreamers?

First, we should advocate for them because they are innocent in regards to immigration law. Erick and other young people like him did not choose to come here. They were brought here by their parents. *They* are not lawbreakers. We can blame many people in our nation for the immigration problems we see all around us. Undocumented adults who entered illegally? Sure. Apathetic, negligent, or corrupt American authorities? Absolutely. The Dreamers? Hardly. They were brought here without their consent and without the ability to navigate the process legally. Justice doesn't punish the innocent.

Second—and I cannot believe I need to say this—children should not be punished for the actions of their parents. It is unjust to punish children for the sins of their fathers and mothers or for the sins of apathetic, negligent, or corrupt American authorities. Justice doesn't punish the innocent.

Legally speaking, American authorities would be within their legal rights to deport Dreamers. But it's hardly a necessary action, as they would *also* be within their legal rights to adjust the application of our laws so that they can show mercy to Dreamers. Our nation has done this many times before in its history and, in doing so, has held together two deeply Christian concepts—justice and mercy. I have yet to hear a legitimate argument that demonstrates how showing mercy to Dreamers undermines a just immigration process.

Third, this is an irreplaceable opportunity to show that America still has some moral fiber. There is some good news on this front: according to multiple recent polls, 75–80 percent of Americans believe we should find a way for Dreamers to stay in the United States legally.[3] That's a consensus we can't seem to muster in just about any other category. With such a large majority in support of protecting the Dreamers, what stops us? Moral cowardice? Apathy? Dirty politics?

The brilliant intellectual Alexis de Tocqueville believed America's greatness stemmed from her goodness, especially the moral fiber of America's cultural institutions. I agree. If we want America to be great, we must help America be morally good. We can do that. But we can't do it by throwing innocent young people into legal limbo. We can't do it by posturing as tough guys on immigration and punishing the people who most need to be protected. We can't do it by forcing Dreamers to spend their lives in the shadows as nonpeople.

In protecting the Dreamers, we will be taking a large stride toward making America good again. I suspect that desire transcends all borders.

Yours,
Bruce

CHAPTER 20

I PLEDGE
ALLEGIANCE . . .

Christian,

I'm sorry to hear that the immigration conversation with your Uncle John *and* the email exchange with Professor Baileywick both went so badly. I felt it a little ironic that both of their insults toward you would be true if they were talking with each other. Baileywick thinks your immigration views are coldhearted and ethnocentric. Uncle John actually appears to be both of those. And Uncle John thinks you are naïvely buying into a system of moral relativism. I couldn't describe Baileywick much better than that.

Fortunately, while their insults seem true of each other, I don't think either is true of you. Of course, expressing a Christian political commitment in today's political climate is liable to leave you feeling politically homeless. It's uncomfortable, but there are worse things. Better to be politically homeless with a good conscience than to be in lockstep conformity with the latest trends at the expense of a clean conscience.

I was eager to get to your next topic (pacifism), but it sounds like you wanted to revisit an issue I mentioned a few letters back—nationalism. As you mentioned in your last letter, you and your dad keep coming back to the idea, and you get the sense—rightly, I think, considering your summaries of the arguments—that the two of you can't seem to agree on a simple definition.

Part of the problem is that various types of nationalism have emerged recently as major contenders on the political scene. Ideological nationalism has always played a role in American politics, but these days it has captured the imagination of Americans in an especially strong way.

There seem to be three major varieties of nationalism today, and they aren't created equal. I'll march through each of them and give you my verdict.

The first variety is "civic nationalism." I'm all for it.

When political scientists refer to civic nationalism, they are describing what many American citizens refer to as "patriotism." A healthy American patriotism believes in the "ideas" that make the United States of America a nation-state—ideas such as religious liberty, freedom of speech, checks and balances on centralized power, and justice and equality for all. Historically, patriotic Americans have often affirmed—albeit inconsistently—the Judeo-Christian moral framework that exercised such a profound influence on our founding ideals and documents.

As I see it, Christians should embrace this sort of patriotism, uniting around the good that is found in our nation's ideals, its founding documents, and its diverse citizens.[1] There is nothing wrong—and everything right—about having a healthy affection for our own nation, in spite of its flaws. A nation is, in some ways, much like a very large family. It's a natural and noble thing to love your family and to expect other people to love theirs. But it's foolish to conclude that your family (or your nation) is beyond critique. Patriotism should never be uncritical. Not only should we love our nation enough to admire and preserve the good in it, but we should also love it enough to resist and stand guard against that which is unjust, evil, and uncivil. Remember what Chesterton said: "When you love a thing, its gladness is a reason for loving it, and its sadness a reason for loving it more."[2] This is the attitude of the civic nationalist—which is to say, the attitude of the patriot.

The second variety is "classic ethno-nationalism." I am categorically opposed.

Classic ethno-nationalism is a type of political racism. When political commentators talk about ethno-nationalists, they are referring to citizens who wish to privilege one ethnic group in our country over all the others. Ethno-nationalists emphasize what they consider to be the exemplary and unique traits of their ethno-nation (the traits may be real *or* imaginary or a mixture of real *and* imaginary). They demand that these traits be preserved and transmitted to future generations. Ethno-nationalists tend to maintain a double standard for justice, privileging the members of the entitled ethnic group over those of other ethnic groups. Ethno-nationalism is the biblical vice of pride applied to entire people groups.

Ethno-nationalism is experiencing a tragic resurgence in America. Or at least it's experiencing more attention. Think about the rise of the so-called "Alt Right," used to refer to a type of white-identity politics that believes in racialism (the need to divide humanity into racial groups) and rejects American conservatism for being a "cuckold movement" (a cuckold is a man whose wife sleeps with other men; likewise, in the Alt-Right telling of the story, white conservatives are wrongfully "in bed with" other races, not only sexually, but socially, culturally, and politically). Not all ethnonationalism is white, of course, but in twenty-first-century America, that's the loudest brand we've got to grapple with. Plus, being a white guy myself, it's important to put some distance between my skin color and this warped ideology.

Now the Alt Right is a loose coalition of white supremacists, white nationalists, antiglobalists, neo-pagans, Internet trolls, and others. Each of these groups has various distinguishing characteristics and priorities, and each group's members have varying degrees of loyalty. Yet they share a determination to prioritize white identity as the ultimate source of identity, something that must be guarded and conserved against all enemies, foreign and domestic. White identity proponents are especially concerned to oppose interracial adoption, interracial marriage, and non-European immigrants.

This white identity is relatively straightforward, but it doesn't fit well with our nation's founding documents. No problem for the Alt Right: they just want to ignore the documents. Richard Spencer, the most prominent leader in the Alt-Right movement, writes, "Our dream is a new society, an ethno-state that would be a gathering point for all Europeans. It would be a new society based on very different ideals than, say, the Declaration of Independence."[3] Who needs annoying obstacles like the Declaration of Independence or petty nuisances such as the American Constitution when you're attempting to create an ethno-state?

The Alt Right and other forms of ethno-nationalism possess an idolatrous view of the world. Their narrative of the world locates a person's *core identity* in relation to his or her ethnic group. It locates *evil* in heteronomous influence or rule (being influenced or ruled by a person external to oneself or one's identity group). It identifies as *saviors* those leaders who can liberate them from being influenced by, or ruled by, other ethnic groups and cultures, and desires a *future* in which clear lines of demarcation exist between ethnic groups.

By way of contrast, the biblical narrative of the world locates a person's *core identity* in relationship to the triune God. It identifies as *evil* any attempt to absolutize some aspect of God's created order (such as sex or money or power or ethnic heritage); any situation in which we trust, love, obey, or fear any aspect of God's creation (such as sex or money or power or ethnic heritage) more than we trust, love, obey, or fear God himself. It identifies Jesus Christ as the *Savior* (Acts 4:12) who will one day *return* to install a new political order in which all worshippers from every ethnic heritage will gather together in unison around his throne (Rev. 5:9).

Given that ethno-nationalism possesses an idolatrous worldview, it should come as no surprise that it also runs afoul of a genuinely Christian view of American politics.[4] Our commitment to human dignity and governmental justice should cause us to view the state as an institution that exercises power with an eye toward justice for all people within its borders and not merely for people of a particular ethnic, socioeconomic, or religious grouping.

Politicial scientist David Koyzis, whom I've mentioned to you before, puts it this way: "The danger of the ethnic variety of nationalism lies in the pursuit of a double standard of justice. When ethnic nationalists come to power in a given state, they privilege the members of their . . . ethnic group over those of other ethnic groups."[5] Christians should reject any attempt to value any of our nation's ethnic groups over another. We should fight racism tooth and nail, in all its forms, not only from the voting booth but also in the public square.

The third variety of nationalism is "economic nationalism." Consider me a skeptic.

In the midst of a global economic recession and large-scale immigration, a type of economic nationalism has arisen in opposition to *globalism*. It doesn't usually stand by itself, latching onto either civic or ethnic nationalism. In fact, this impulse toward economic nationalism is so strong that during the 2016 presidential election cycle, it was a major factor in reorienting the long-standing political divide in our nation from "conservative vs. progressive" to "open country vs. closed country." Economic nationalism stakes out a fairly isolationist economic position by closing the borders, restricting free trade, and intervening in the domestic economy.

Economic nationalism is a bit more of a mixed bag than the previous two types of nationalism. On the positive side, the intentions behind economic nationalism are generally good. Economic nationalists want to help blue-collar and financially disadvantaged citizens who have borne the brunt of globalization's negative side effects. And they should be commended for recognizing the extent of the problem before many of us did. Globalization, as Christopher Caldwell and R. R. Reno have pointed out, benefits America's economic winners at the same time as it benefits immigrants from the poorer nations. Both groups, despite very different experiences, profit from immigration, outsourcing, and free-trade agreements.[6] America's economic losers, however, don't see any of the same benefits.

Consider immigration, for example: in a globalized economy, poor immigrants from outside the United States can come to our country and get paying jobs. Net win for them, net win for wealthier Americans, who get less expensive labor and other benefits. Meanwhile, poorer Americans get a fresh wave of competitors for the jobs that put food on their own tables.

Good intentions, however, aren't all that is necessary for good policy. We need to evaluate economic nationalism based on probable outcomes: will economically nationalist policies end up helping the disadvantaged, or will they harm them in the long run? Obviously its advocates think it will help. But the evidence is mixed. Most economists suspect it will create at least as many problems as it solves. That seems like the right assessment. Yes, international trade poses a challenge for economic stability, especially for working-class Americans. But we should consider that the solution might not be economic isolationism, on the one hand, or more federal intervention in the economy, on the other.[7]

I'm willing to be convinced that economic nationalism is a good idea for the American poor. But I haven't been yet.

I'm sure you could spin out a few other variations of nationalism, but those three seem the most relevant in our time. Support the first, oppose the second, and ask critical questions of the third. Don't hold me accountable if your dad parses the situation differently, but I'm optimistic this three-fold distinction will serve you well as you talk with him. And with any luck it will help our country too.

Yours,

Bruce

CHAPTER 21

PRAY FOR PEACE, PREPARE FOR WAR

Christian,

And here I thought the big issue with your dad was going to be about nationalism. It turns out that once you defined your terms, the two of you weren't that far apart. But then you tried to press your advantage and prove that the only viable international posture is a pacifist one. Unsurprisingly, your dad came at you with both barrels.

It looks like I'm going to side with your dad on this one. He's right when he says your pacifism is unrealistic. To add insult to injury, I'll add that pacifist ideology causes its adherents to act in unloving and—gasp!—unbiblical ways.

It's not that I impugn your motives. You're right to seek a better world, one in which people do not die violently at the end of a gun barrel. You and I agree on that one; pacifists and nonpacifists usually do. As one of my favorite nonpacifists, George Washington, put it, "My first wish is to see this plague of mankind, war, banished from the earth." The problem is that the world will not be free from violence until Jesus returns to set the world aright. In the meantime we must be prepared to "fight fire with fire" if and when our nation comes under attack.

But I'm getting ahead of myself. Let me take a moment to outline three mind-sets concerning war and peace. I hinted at this a little when you brought up gun control, but it's time for a deeper dive.

First, *pacifism*. Ostensibly, this is you. (I say "ostensibly" because I suspect that you may be inconsistent in the way you hold this view. More on that in a moment.) Pacifists view deadly force as inherently evil. They refuse to use deadly force or justify the actions of other people who use it. Consistent pacifists resist lethal force just as much when it is legal as when it is vigilante. Thus, they oppose individual gun ownership, but they also work against capital punishment or the use of deadly force within the police or the military. Pacifists generally acknowledge that people should be allowed to resist the force of others, but they encourage people to resist in nonviolent ways.

Christian pacifists often cite Jesus' statements, "Blessed are the peacemakers" and "Love your enemies" to argue that God wants us to love him by setting aside lesser loves of blood and soil (Matt. 5:9, 38–46). They point out that Jesus rebuked Peter for drawing his sword and conclude that we also should refuse to use weapons (Matt. 26:52). They rightly emphasize that the Bible repeatedly urges us to live at peace with each other (Mark 9:50; 1 Cor. 7:15) and conclude that we should never fight a war in order to achieve peace. You put it well in your letter: "We follow a Lord who encountered violence all around him. He had all the power in the universe to oppose it, but he chose instead to pursue peace. If Jesus really is the way, the truth, and the life, I don't see how following the Lord of life can lead any sane Christian to pursue someone else's death."

I've rarely met a pacifist who lacks verve, and you're no different. But I think you're approaching the biblical text with one eye closed. To put it plainly, Jesus was not a pacifist. He used violence to cleanse the temple (John 2:15–16), told his followers that he came to bring a sword (Matt. 10:34), commanded his disciples to carry swords (Luke 22:36), and promises to use deadly force against his enemies one day (Rev. 19:11–15). He (and his disciples after him) interacted with many military men, and not once did he even hint that their profession was inherently sinful. Beyond the example of Jesus, the Bible as a whole makes clear that it is acceptable—and even incumbent upon us—to use violence in some instances.

Additionally, as I hinted above, most pacifists simply aren't consistent enough for me to take their position seriously. Politically, they're inconsistent because they often allow that the government has to use violence in certain cases, but they opt out of that participation themselves. Biblically, they're usually inconsistent in the way they apply Jesus' commands in the Sermon on the Mount. They take him very literally when he says we are to "turn the other cheek," but I wonder if they apply the same literal vigor to Jesus' statement to give money to *all* who demand it, especially unjustly (Matt. 5:39–40).

On the other side of the spectrum, we have the *crusade* mentality. You seem to think your dad is in this category. I'm not so sure. (Uncle John, on the other hand . . .) Crusaders view war as a righteous way of eradicating evil ways of life and imposing their own "good" way of life upon another group of people. Crusaders are always ideological, though not necessarily religious. They are led by individuals or groups that wield religious authority (e.g., a Muslim imam) or ideological authority (e.g., Josef Stalin). Because crusaders view their cause as righteous, they rarely exercise restraint against enemies. They are on the side of the angels and fighting against evil itself, so capitulation shows not only weakness of power but of morality. Thus they seek total annihilation of evil so they can impose their own ideal social order. Since evil can't *actually* be fully eradicated, crusade tends to be a permanent state of affairs.

Christian crusaders—I hate the phrase as much as you do—often point to crusading in the Bible, such as the war of vengeance Moses waged against the Midianites (Num. 31:1–54), the crusade Joshua led to claim the promised land for Israel (Josh. 1:1–7), and Jesus' promise to lead a final crusade to defeat his enemies and institute a one-world government (Rev. 19:11–21). You can probably see the wacky interpretive leaps they need to make their case. In each of the biblical instances of crusade, God himself commanded or even led the crusade: God alone has the right to stamp out evil whenever or wherever he sees it. We do not.

This is where I think you've got a point with the example of Jesus. His strategy to eradicate evil was not (at least in his first coming) through violence and force. He initiated a kingdom that operates under different principles of power than the world uses. We don't kill the deepest roots of evil by killing people.

In the end pacifism and crusaderism are both too simple to be helpful in real life. Even though they appear to be polar opposites, they share a major ideological flaw: they are idealists. They seek perfection in the here and now. Pacifists envision a nonviolent world ushered in by their own nonviolent example; crusaders envision a nonviolent world imposed by their own weapons. Both visions are wrong because idealism is wrong. Idealism assumes our actions will usher in the kingdom of God. That's different from faithfully following Jesus and awaiting his return, as we realists do.

I am a peace-loving proponent of what is called a *just-war* ethic. A just war ethic begins with the realistic recognition that we cannot eradicate evil. But we can and should do what we can to contain it. For that reason legitimate authorities (like the military or the police) must sometimes use deadly force to protect good against evil, but they should only do so within certain parameters. I don't like daydreaming about anyone getting killed, but as a Christian realist, I like this view. It recognizes that we live in a fallen world in which war cannot be eradicated (Matt. 24:6), that God holds rulers responsible for maintaining order and engaging in just war (Rom. 13:4), and that Jesus expected his disciples to carry weapons in case of need (Luke 22:36).

At this point you might be thinking, *That sounds well and good in theory, but I've seen a lot of "just war" talk that sounds a lot like crusaderism.* And you're right. Many of the powerful people in America's political parties use just-war rhetoric but follow crusader ideology. So let's bypass the sound-bite descriptions of just war offered by politicians and media personalities and, instead, summarize the criteria that must be met in order for a war to be "just."

I first encountered these principles in an introductory ethics course with just-war theorist Daniel Heimbach,[1] who summarizes and works out the implications of Augustine's "just war" point of view. I hope these principles will bring clarity to your thinking the way they did to mine. The first set of criteria is referred to as *jus ad bellum,* meaning principles guiding a nation's decision about whether to become engaged in war. These are:

1. *Just cause.* A nation should not go to war unless it is correcting a *specific* injustice; in other words it may not go to war to "eradicate evil" or "promote democracy."
2. *Competent authority.* A decision to go to war should not be made by anybody other than the people who are ultimately responsible for maintaining security and civil order. Vigilante justice isn't just.
3. *Comparative justice.* A nation must weigh whether going to war might cause more injustice than existed in the first place; a nation must not cause more injustice going to war than would be suffered not going to war.
4. *Right intention.* A nation may not engage in war to punish or humiliate its enemies or to seek to glorify and empower itself; it may only engage in war to restore a previous state of peace in the sense of civil order. This is a close cousin to number one.
5. *Last resort.* A nation must exhaust all realistic nonviolent alternatives before going to war; a nation should always prefer solutions that do not involve the use of deadly force.
6. *Probability of success.* A nation should not engage in war unless it has a realistic chance of victory; otherwise it wastes lives and resources.
7. *Proportionality of projected results.* A nation must count the cost before going to war; if the costs of victory are more than the costs of nonengagement, the nation should not go to war.
8. *Right spirit.* A nation must not go to war in a spirit of ideological zeal, blood thirst, or hatred; it must engage in war with no sense of satisfaction other

than that it is restoring peace, maintaining order, and protecting the innocent.

The second set of criteria is referred to as *jus in bello*, meaning principles guiding a nation's actions in the midst of an ongoing war:

1. *Proportionality in the use of force.* A nation's military must limit its use of force to the amount required to gain legitimate military goals. Killing ten thousand people in retaliation for an attack that killed twenty is disproportionate and, thus, unjust.
2. *Discrimination.* A nation's military must distinguish between combatants and noncombatants, taking care not to target noncombatant lives or property.
3. *Avoidance of evil means.* A nation's military should never employ evil means, such as rape, pillage, desecration of holy places, destruction of crops, or targeting of civilians. This is a tricky one, but the spirit here is to counteract the ever-present notion that in war "anything goes."
4. *Good faith.* A nation's military must treat enemy combatants as human beings rather than as subhuman beings; it must treat them with dignity and decency.
5. *Probability of success (in bello).* Once military command loses any realistic hope of victory, it should arrange for an honorable surrender.
6. *Probability of projected results (in bello).* Once military command realizes continued fighting would cost more than winning is worth, it should either stop fighting in such a costly manner or stop fighting altogether.
7. *Right spirit (in bello).* Military personnel should love their enemies by engaging the enemy in a spirit

of regret rather than one of hatred, blood thirst, or delight. Even if we know our cause to be right, none of us should *enjoy* taking the lives of others.

You may read over that and think, "Well, if *that's* the case, I can't think of many just wars." You're right that many nations go to war unjustly even while using just-war rhetoric. Even though I believe a legitimate "just war" ethic is the best way to navigate war and peace in a fallen world, I acknowledge it's a practice filled with pitfalls. Still it is the only view that takes into account the biblical teaching that evil and war will not be eradicated until Jesus returns. We must sometimes wage war responsibly in order to correct a specific injustice and restore peace. In the words of General Norman Schwarzkopf, "Any soldier worth his salt should be antiwar. And still there are things worth fighting for."[2]

Now, my little lists of criteria are tidy and sanitary. But as you can imagine, applying all of this is hardly simple.

For example, there's a lively debate about whether the "just cause" criterion should be expanded to include "preventive" strikes. Not a *preemptive* strike but a *preventive* one. A preemptive strike is one in which a nation becomes aware of specific confirmed evidence that an adversary has set in motion an attack and, in response, the nation launches its own strike to preempt the attack. Preemptive attacks recognize that you don't have to fire the first shot to be the aggressor.

That scenario is different from a *preventive* strike. In a preventive strike, Nation A declares that Nation B is evil and will "probably" or "assuredly" do evil things in the future. Based on this assumption, Nation A attacks evil Nation B. This may sound similar to a preemptive strike, but it really isn't. In a preventive strike the only criteria for aggression is a perceived threat. Just about every aggressor in history has used "perceived threats" as the grounds for his crusading. This isn't just the first step but a running jump down the slippery slope of the crusade mentality.

Or so I argue. Some just-war theorists disagree with me on this. They are wrong, but they persist.

Consider, as another example, the ongoing debate about the use of "enhanced interrogation techniques," or, as they called it in the old days, torture. Some ethicists, politicians, and military personnel find torture useful in order to extract important information from enemy combatants. This is a dangerous trend, and we need to approach the issue with an enormous amount of caution. In many instances we must categorically oppose torture. For instance, are we warranted in torturing a POW's wife or children in order to force a confession? Absolutely not. But are we warranted in waterboarding a POW to extract information? Some say yes. Others say no. And a bunch of us land in the middle with a strong maybe. It depends on how certain we are that the prisoner knows critical information, how much is riding on gaining that information, and whether other less-violent methods could be just as effective in obtaining the information in a timely manner. Even if we know for certain that the outcome will be beneficial, we've still got to grapple with the *jus in bello* principle of "good faith" mentioned above. Is it possible to subject another person to pain we would *never* choose for ourselves and still be treating that person with dignity and decency?

I wish I had more time to engage some of the other just-war questions, too. Are drone strikes ethical? Can nonstate actors engage in a just war? Which of America's recent military conflicts meet the criteria for a just war? Does the "age of terrorism" change the rules of conflict? How should we think about nuclear weapons? I think there are some good answers to these questions, but we'll have to discuss them in person some time. Chances are by the time we get around to discussing them, there will be new questions to ask. It's a tangled web, for sure.

For now, I hope I've at least given the just-war position a fighting shot with you.

Yours,

Bruce

CHAPTER 22

RESTORING THE SELF

Christian,

Your editor at CCNN likes to toss you softballs, huh? An opinion piece on whether transgender people should be allowed to serve in the military. I'll leave you to answer that specific question, but I want to equip you to think about the transgender *movement* and how we should treat transgender *persons*. From your letter I can tell you are uneasy about these questions, and both of them must be answered prior to public policy questions.

Let's start by clarifying such terms as *sex*, *gender*, *gender identity*, *gender dysphoria*, and *transgender*.

Sex is the physical identification a person has from birth. It distinguishes male and female from one another via qualities such as the person's anatomical design, chromosomes, and hormones. This is the clearest distinction in the bunch as it's biologically based.

Gender is similar to *sex* but carries social and cultural baggage with it. I've heard it said that you *have* a sex but you *do* a gender. That can be overstated, but it makes an important point. While *sex* distinguishes between biological males and females, *gender* describes the group of behaviors that are typically associated with masculinity and femininity. These can vary across cultures and times. For instance, men in other countries often hold hands to show friendship; they rarely do in the United States.

Gender identity is a term used to describe a person's conception of identity—either as masculine, feminine, or (recently) some other option. Since gender is more fluid than sex, the idea here is that people may choose to align their cultural behavior with a gender that does not match their biological sex. Until recently this only expressed itself in behaviors (like cross-dressing). But with modern technology, there is more of a push to force our biology to bow to our gender identity through hormone treatments and surgeries.

Within the transgender community, the key distinction is between those who are *transgender* and those who are *cisgender.* The latter term refers to anyone whose gender identity aligns with their biological sex (born male, considers himself male). The former refers to those who feel that they are *not* what their biological sex says.

Gender dysphoria describes the psychological stress that occurs when individuals experience a conflict between the gender they were assigned at birth and the gender with which they identify. They were born men but don't *feel* like men. People who suffer from gender dysphoria do not necessarily identify as *transgender,* as that label indicates not only the emotional experience but also a desire to act in certain ways. In other words, a person might experience conflict within but may not take the step of publicly switching gender identity.

All of this is pretty historically novel, so let's see if we can evaluate gender dysphoria and transgenderism in light of God's teaching set forth in the Bible.

The first significant biblical teaching is found in the first chapter of the first book of the Bible: "He created him in the image of God; he created them male and female" (Gen. 1:27). God created human beings in his image as the culmination of the created order, with the distinction between male and female being essential to his design. He created men and women with equal dignity and worth but with different characteristics. The differences are intended by God, and they are not interchangeable.

This means God is the ultimate authority in the transgender debate. He designed human beings as male or female, and we should tremble to override the Creator's design. Attempts to override the Creator's design, in truth, are futile. It cannot be done. When people reject God's design for them, they are in a very real way rejecting God. Adam and Eve were designed to have fellowship with God and obey his commandments. The moment they deviated from this and pursued an alternate plan, human history began its spiral toward destruction. Rejecting God's design is a weighty matter.

God created the world in certain ways, and when we attempt to nullify or suppress that design, we will meet with frustration and failure. Despite the growing technological advances in our time, our bodies have limits and are not endlessly pliable. We are *designed* beings; no matter how hard we try to suppress God's design, we cannot.

A good example of this reality is the 2014 women's mixed martial arts bout between Tamikka Brents and Fallon Fox. During a two-minute beating, Brents suffered a concussion, an orbital bone fracture, and needed seven staples to close wounds on her head. "I've fought a lot of women and have never felt the strength that I felt in a fight as I did that night," said Brents.[1]

As it turns out, Fallon Fox wasn't born female. She is a biological male who identifies as transgender. Brents thought Fox had an unfair advantage. "I can't answer whether it's because she was born a man or not because I'm not a doctor," said Brents. "I can only say, I've never felt so overpowered ever in my life, and I am an abnormally strong female in my own right."

I'm not surprised that the first instances of transgenderism in athletics are flowing in this direction. I haven't heard of any biological women who claim to be men in order to compete against men. Nor do I expect to. The physical differences are so overwhelming that women cannot compete effectively against professional male fighters. (Although I can imagine Tamikka Brents puttin' a whuppin' on any number of men who are not professional fighters.) Most sports activities are segregated by sex because of biological reality. On average, men are physically stronger than women because we have, on average, more total muscle mass. Men also have greater cardiovascular reserve, greater lung volume per body mass, denser and stronger bones, tendons, and ligaments. These factors give men a natural physical advantage over women in sports. This physical difference doesn't mean men are, ontologically, *better or more important* than women. But it should be obvious that they're different. And that is why, until recently, public policy made these biological distinctions the basis for issuing sex-segregated policies concerning restroom usage and housing policies in college.

The second significant teaching follows on the heels of the first. As I just mentioned, Adam and Eve decided to reject God so they could control their own lives (Gen. 3). It didn't go well for them, just as it doesn't go well for us when we usurp his authority. At the bottom of our rejection of God is our false belief that we will not be satisfied unless we act on our heart's desires. That rejection is now part of the warp and woof of our society, which is actively encouraging the next generation to "look within" for true meaning, to "follow your heart" and "be true to yourself" in order to find freedom. It sounds appealing, but it's the same lie Adam and Eve bought into in the garden.

It is a dangerous mistake for those who experience gender dysphoria to take the concrete step of trying to change their gender. Although it is not a sin to experience confusion about one's gender, it is wrong to try to alter the gender identity assigned by God himself. And like all deviations from God's design, it promises life but delivers death. The current media depiction of transgenderism is one of liberation from bondage: trapped in the wrong body, transgender people are given a chance—through medical marvels—to become who they really are. But actual experience shows that gender dysphoria goes much deeper than this. It can't be "fixed" with surgery, and "pro-science" citizens won't help things by pretending that it can.

People with gender dysphoria may have a unique struggle, but in the most important ways, they are like the rest of us. They are born with broken bodies, just like you and me. They experience suffering and temptation, just like you and me. The answer lies not in ignoring suffering or succumbing to temptation but in offering up our broken bodies to God. This may not be easy, but it is the only path to true freedom and life.

That's the third significant biblical teaching: God offers to save us from our sin and eventually to restore us entirely. In other words, he makes one offer we can take him up on immediately: he will save us from our sins and transform our hearts in the here and now. And he makes a promise for the future, that he will return one day to fix the brokenness of this world and the brokenness of our minds and bodies.

For a person experiencing gender dysphoria, this means that God offers to transform their hearts so they can love

God. It means it's possible to live according to the way God designed them and their bodies. This won't be magical, and it certainly won't be immediate. God doesn't promise he'll *right now* put an end to their dysphoria, to their desires to live like a member of the opposite sex. That may persist until their dying day. But he does promise that if they'll wait patiently for him to return and set the world aright, they will finally experience life without the temptation to live contrary to God's design.

Now, how should we treat transgender persons?

We should love them. Jesus made clear that we should love each other and that this—our love for each other—is the sign that we are actually Christians. The apostle John made this crystal clear when he wrote, "If anyone says, 'I love God,' and yet hates his brother or sister, he is a liar. For the person who does not love his brother or sister whom he has seen cannot love God whom he has not seen" (1 John 4:20).

As Christian ethicist Andrew Walker notes in his book *God and the Transgender Debate*, loving transgender persons involves dignity, empathy, compassion, and patience.[2] We recognize the God-given dignity of a transgender person who is created in God's image, possesses great worth, and is deserving of honor and respect. We work hard to empathize with them, trying to see life from their perspective. We have compassion on them, befriending them and walking with them through their life experiences and struggles. And we have patience, entering into their lives to love them for the long haul. Love is hard work, but we Christians should be known for it, particularly among those who disagree with us.

But love for a transgender person also entails telling the truth. We cannot afford to send signals that we approve of their living with a gender identity different from their God-given sex. This isn't unique to transgenderism, either. Loving others doesn't mean we necessarily approve of their life goals or actions. In fact, the most loving thing we can do for people who are making sinful decisions is to warn them about the truth. For those people experiencing gender dysphoria or identifying as transgender, that means telling them the truth about God's design for gender. We don't shout them down by calling them freaks, but we lift them up by showing them that they are made in God's image, that their sin doesn't need to define them, and that God has a glorious future for them.

One of Christianity's most compelling teachers is Vaughan Roberts, a prominent Anglican pastor who has experienced same-sex attraction as long as he can remember. Contrary to the narrative of the LGBT community, which would encourage him to "be true to himself," Roberts has chosen to be celibate because he wishes to live according to God's design. He knows what it is, from experience, to live according to a pattern that doesn't "feel" right. But Roberts urges us to take a different view of our lives, which he calls "art restoration." He explains:

> If you see a work of art and you're asked to restore it, you don't look at it and say, "Well, I think he would look much nicer with a pair of spectacles." Or, "this scene would look better with a car instead of a hay cart." To do that is to break the code of the art restorer.
>
> Art restorers respect the work, and know that their job is to bring out the artist's original intention.[3]

If we truly want to help people who suffer from gender dysphoria, we'll help them endure suffering and resist sin as it relates to their bodies. We'll also help them walk the path of discipleship in thousands of ways *unrelated* to their gender dysphoria. God doesn't save people from homosexuality or transgenderism; he saves us from sin, and that's universal.

Persons with gender dysphoria are like the rest of us—they need hope. As we introduce them to Christ, who alone can transform their hearts and eventually restores their bodies, we give them hope. As they seek their identity in Christ (1 Cor. 6:17), they will be able to find healing for their brokenness. Even though the Lord doesn't promise to immediately take away our sinful desires or heal us from our present suffering, he does promise to transform our hearts and, later, transform our broken bodies.

In light of the biblical picture, how should we respond to transgenderism as a social, cultural, and political movement?

In a word, we should resist it. It is bad for society and bad for individuals. As the great sociologist Philip Rieff argued, American society is in the midst of an unprecedented experiment in building society apart from religion. One of the primary ways we've done this is through sex and gender. By untethering sex from marriage, we have enabled the normalization of no-fault divorce, the explosive spread of STDs, the death of sixty million babies in the womb, and an epidemic divorce rate. And by celebrating the severing gender identity from God-given sex, we will likewise reap a psychological, social, cultural, and political whirlwind.

We must be especially vigilant in protecting our children from the transgender revolution. Many of the most powerful cultural influencers in our nation not only encourage transgenderism but make heroes out of people who publicly identify with a different sex from the one assigned at birth. First and foremost, my heart breaks because of the lie this proclaims to those suffering from gender dysphoria. They need to know that transgenderism doesn't deliver on its promises. But we also need to protect our children by making clear that transgenderism is against God's good design for human flourishing.

For most of us, this still seems like a strange discussion and one that may not have tangible results. But ideas have consequences. Already we are seeing many physicians who are willing to give hormonal treatments to gender dysphoric children in order to delay puberty. But as a recent study shows, "Regardless of the good intentions of the physicians and parents, to expose young people to such treatments is to endanger them."[4] In fact, these types of medical treatments are harmful and even abusive, considering that upwards of 80 percent of gender-dysphoric children grow comfortable in their bodies and no longer experience dysphoria.[5]

I wish that all of the contemporary political posturing wouldn't color this issue so much because there are real people whose lives are affected by it. The more transgenderism is blindly held up as a panacea, the more disappointed people will be when the cure doesn't hold up.

I've made a lot of distinctions in this letter, but I want to end by making an important point of commonality. Those with gender dysphoria experience a deep, personal angst. They struggle to live obediently before God. I sympathize with their experience, even though I can't fully understand it.

But I also recognize that God uses emotional turmoil to tune us in to a spiritual reality that many of us can too easily ignore. People with gender dysphoria *know* that something isn't right in their experience of the world. Would that we all had this clarity of vision. Because Jesus only heals those who know they are broken and only comforts those who admit they are hurting.

That should be every last one of us.

Yours,

Bruce

CHAPTER 23

FAKE NEWS AND
ALTERNATIVE FACTS

Christian,

I read your article about transgender people serving in the military. The content was solid, but I was more impressed with your tone. You managed to display deep compassion for people with gender dysphoria, yet at the same time showed the problems with transgender ideology. A few letters back I gave you a little warning with the words of Justice Scalia's: "Attack ideas, not people. Some very good people have some very bad ideas." It seems that since then you have become a Scalia disciple. Well done.

I also read your last letter to me, which was exactly right. Out of the cornucopia of rotten fruit offered in recent American culture, one of the most putrid is "fake news." The 2016 election cycle brought the situation to a head. We learned that a number of websites plagiarized the look of mainstream media outlets in order to spread patently false stories. Readers were more likely to believe the stories because they seemed to have come from trusted news outlets.

This realization caused a firestorm of controversies, including allegations that Russia waged a misinformation campaign in order to sway the U.S. presidential election,[1] a recent Italian referendum,[2] and most recently the French presidential election.[3] (Facebook suspended thirty thousand fake "Internet robot" accounts in the lead up to France's presidential elections.[4]) Facebook was accused of being complicit by providing a prominent platform for false information. As a result, CEO Mark Zuckerberg has spent a considerable amount of time defending his company. We live in odd times.

You also pointed out that in our letter exchanges I've spent a lot of time criticizing silliness on the Left. I would like to consider myself an equal opportunity offender, but I suppose you've got a point. In light of that fact, I'll start off today's letter by exposing some silliness on the Right.

During the 2016 election, radio host Ira Glass interviewed his Uncle Lenny, an eighty-one-year-old retired plastic surgeon who gets all his news from conservative outlets. During the interview Uncle Lenny made several audacious claims about President Obama.[5] (It makes me wonder if your Uncle John and his Uncle Lenny might be kin.)

Uncle Lenny started by boldly declaring that Obama has "played more rounds of golf than any president in history." (Not true: Ike Eisenhower played three times as much, and Woodrow Wilson four.) He continued by saying, "[Obama] claims to have run the *Harvard Law Review*. Why didn't he write a single article for them?" (Obama did, in fact, edit the *Harvard Law Review*. And as editors do, he wrote unsigned pieces for it.) Then Uncle Lenny went for broke, claiming, "No one in Obama's law school class can ever remember having seen him there." Glass, who appears to possess the patience of a saint, calmly pointed out that a friend of his knew Obama when they were in law school together.

Uncle Lenny, not having a ready reply, shifted fields. He declared that President Obama chose to ignore laws about deporting people in the country illegally. Glass, still attempting to keep the discussion within the realm of recordable evidence, pointed out that Obama had actually deported more people than any other president. Do you remember the number from a few letters back? Nearly three million.[6] Uncle Lenny, painted into a corner for the last time, retreated to his happy place: "I don't believe that, Ira, for one minute. I don't believe that."[7] You've got to admire Uncle Lenny's dedication.

After the interview with Uncle Lenny, Glass concluded, "Facts do not have a fighting chance against this right-wing fable." Glass is right. I think he's ignoring the fact that the Left has unassailable fables of its own. But he's right. People today seem more prone to stick to their position even *after* being shown evidence to the contrary. If it doesn't fit within my view, it must not be true.

That's our world today—filled with "fake news," "alternative facts," a "posttruth" approach to reality. There are plenty of people like "Uncle Lenny" who have—wittingly or unwittingly—embraced our posttruth world. In 2016 Oxford dictionaries even announced that it had selected *posttruth* as its international Word of the Year. Oxford defines *posttruth* as "relating to or denoting circumstances in which objective facts are less influential in shaping public opinion than appeals to emotion and personal belief."[8] The Oxford definition only reveals part of the problem. The deeper root of the problem is that many people in our posttruth world convey false information *on purpose* in order to accomplish some personal, professional, or political goal.

I like the way Christian philosopher Ravi Zacharias puts it:

Here is the post-mortem. Post-truth as a phenomenon is not new. Just as postmodern is neither post nor modern but existed in the first conversation at creation's dawn—"Has God spoken?"—so also post-truth is actually rebellion right from the beginning. "Has God given us his word?" The answer to that question spelled life or death.[9]

Now, before we continue, let's be clear: it's perfectly fine for us to appeal to emotion when we are making the case for our views. Aristotle, for instance, recognized this in *On Rhetoric*, the first and most influential book on communication. He categorized the essential elements of communication as *logos* (argument from reason), *pathos* (appeal to emotion), and *ethos* (the persuasive appeal of one's character). A good argument combines all three elements: it aims for truth, it connects with the emotions, and it is made by a person of good character. So an appeal to emotion is only wrong when it ignores or obscures the facts.

But that is exactly what some people do. Jesus pointed this out in a first-century version of an "Uncle Lenny" conversation—the parable of Lazarus and the rich man. In this parable Jesus makes the point that, if a man were to rise from the dead, people would not believe the evidence if they had already decided not to take God at his word. In other words, if people have already made up their minds, they will ignore the evidence.

So the posttruth mind-set has been around since at least the days of Jesus. But why has it become such a problem today? I see three major reasons.

First, we are experiencing a breakdown in the authority of the national media outlets and other information sources. Historically, Americans have relied on pyramid-shaped, hierarchical authorities, such as the *Encyclopedia Britannica* (knowledge articles), colleges and universities (education and research), and national newspapers (news and opinion).

On the whole we trusted these authorities because they had a system of checks and balances that included authoritative fact-checkers and editors who made it likely they conveyed information reliably. Walter Cronkite could sign off his news stories with, "And that's the way it is," and we nodded along.

However, as our society has polarized politically, and as the Internet has flattened the information world into more of a "pancake" than a "pyramid" shape, our locus of trust has shifted. Now we tend to trust open-source information outlets like Wikipedia, special-interest websites, and blogs. We trust these "pancake" authorities based on the reputation of their distributed accountability system. We trust—for the most part—the accuracy of information in a Wikipedia article because it has been filtered through hundreds or even thousands of self-appointed editors and is backed by an error-correction system that is open to public accountability.

This shift from "pyramid" to "pancake," however, isn't as simple as a shift from news hierarchy to news democracy. Most information distributed by "pancake" authorities is produced by "pyramid" authorities, so it's not surprising that we find many of the same merits (and drawbacks) with each approach.

The more interesting question is not "*Which* information outlets can we trust?" but "*How* should we determine which outlets are trustworthy?" As I see it, the initial and primary basis for almost all authority is reputation (what Aristotle would call *ethos*). We trust the entries in the *Encyclopedia Britannica* not because we know the editors personally but because millions of other people, including renowned experts, also trust the accuracy of the entries. If a *Britannica* article has errors, we reason, somebody will report it to *Britannica*, and the article will be corrected. In other words, we trust that an error-correction system similar to the one at Wikipedia is also in effect at *Britannica*.

Encyclopedias, though, tend to deal with facts that are more or less established. What about information that is highly contested or open to interpretation—like current events? In such instances we tend to side with the interpretation taken by people who share our own political ideology, religious view, or social perspective. In addition, we often end up getting all of our information from outlets that confirm what we already believe. In other words, we end up placing ourselves in an "echo chamber," a situation in which our beliefs and perceptions are echoed back to us by people who have the same beliefs and perceptions.

Second, we can't just blame the media. It is human nature to look for news and opinion from outlets that affirm us and our views—over against the views of the stupid and bad people on the other side of the aisle. We don't like to have our view of the world challenged or called into question. Part of this is understandable and natural. If I have chosen my beliefs intentionally and believe them with conviction, it makes sense that I would resist viewpoints that challenge those beliefs.

If we want to have a civil society, we need to be grown-ups and get used to this kind of cognitive dissonance. If we don't, we're part of the problem. We can't lay all of the blame on the media when we rush to get our information from special-interest websites, political spinmeisters, conspiracy theorists, Facebook shares, and email forwards whose views systematically confirm our own biases. The media outlets may be biased, but they make their money off of us average folk. If we stopped eating what they dish out, they'd change their menu.

Third, new technology enables false information to spread instantaneously and globally. Back in the nineteenth century, when fake news emerged as a phenomenon in the Western newspaper industry, the news couldn't spread as quickly or as broadly.[10] But fake news today isn't spread primarily via newspapers delivered to our doorstep. It is delivered by websites and social media that enable it to be instantaneously accessible and potentially viral. Additionally, analytics software allows information outlets to know which types of stories get the most "clicks." Websites with the most clicks make the most money from advertisers. Websites with the most money stay in business. Can you guess what all of that adds up to? An information ecosystem that rewards sensational articles. Don't have a true sensational article on offer at the moment? Well, let's leave truth for another day and make our money today.

Put those three reasons together, and you can begin to see why fake news is such a problem. We're losing faith in our authoritative media outlets, seeing the rise of a host of other dodgy "news" sources, ignoring facts that don't fit our assumptions, and gobbling up sensational garbage with gusto.

Pretty depressing, no? But let's not despair. We haven't yet reached the American Dialect Society's 2016 Word of the Year situation—a "dumpster fire." There are some fairly easy ways "We the People" can fight back against fake news. I offer five.

First, we should do some basic research regarding the news sources we consume. If you are reading a Web-based article, look at the URL to make sure the website is not posing as a mainstream outlet when in fact it is not. Look at the website's description of itself to make sure it is not a satire site. Google the author to determine his or her credibility. Find some fact-check websites that might be able to verify the claims in the article. This isn't as hard as it sounds, and it would save us a lot of headaches.

Consider a real scenario. During the 2016 election cycle, the *Nevada County Scooper* wrote that Vice President-elect Mike Pence had made a surprise announcement crediting gay conversion therapy for saving his marriage. The article was shared via hundreds of thousands of email inboxes, Facebook accounts, and Twitter feeds. But the gullible readers who believed this satirical article could have easily known that it was satire if they had just Googled "Nevada County Scooper"; within the first few links is an article revealing that the article is fake news.[11]

Second, we should beware of confirmation bias. As human beings, we tend to agree with something if it confirms something we already believe about the world. So fake news taps into our confirmation bias by wrapping its falsehoods into a framework of beliefs that we already accept. So, for example, if a reader believes that George W. Bush or Barack Obama is a bad person, a fake news writer can establish a backdrop of credibility with the reader by wrapping an outlandishly false claim about Bush or Obama in a blanket of real negative facts and real established opinions. If you walk away from an article thinking, "See! I *knew* it!" you might want to double-check the details.

Third, we must remind ourselves continually that there are people out there who actively and intentionally lie, exaggerate, and misinform in order to achieve their social, cultural, and political agendas. These people are found pretty evenly across the Left and the Right, and they prey on our "confirmation bias" to further their own agenda. The real rub here is to beware of *our* own social, cultural, and political agendas as keenly as we are aware of *other people's* agendas.

Fourth, we should access our news and opinions from a variety of outlets, resisting the temptation to live in an echo chamber. Instead of combining a pervasive distrust of media in general with a loyal allegiance to one outlet in particular, we should expose ourselves to a variety of media outlets, using our critical faculties to find the truth amid the competing voices.

Fifth, we should find ways to support honest journalists and media outlets. More than any other institution, the press is tasked with guarding truth in the public square. As Peter Stockland put it recently, "Journalists are no more (and, admittedly, no less) than citizens who have taken it upon themselves to pass [trustworthy] information on to their fellow citizens—and therefore obliged to respect the common good, the common order, and, above all, the common law."[12] For that reason, we should reward news outlets, reporters, and opinion writers who are serious about guarding the truth. Send an email thanking them. Leave a comment on their Web article. Commit to read their articles or watch their show regularly. Once you get out of college and have more than a couple bucks in your pocket, you might even support them financially.

Well, that's enough for now. Let's demand *honesty and integrity* from journalists, writers, and pundits. Let's demand *wisdom and discernment* from ourselves and fellow citizens as we imbibe news and opinion. And let's talk again soon.

Yours,
Bruce

PART 3

A CHRISTIAN HOPE FOR AMERICAN POLITICS

CHAPTER 24

IF YOU CAN KEEP IT
(REPRISE)

Christian,

Welcome back to school! Despite your protestations to the contrary, I know that deep down you missed the frenzied stress of campus life. After all, you're back at *Dupont* (try to hear that with all of the *gravitas* and pomp with which your professors say it), which is no place to be caught slacking.

That's not to say that you should be spending all of your time studying. There are three essential aspects to college life—academics, sleep, and social life. The pace of life at Dupont gives you just enough time to choose two. Choose wisely.

Now that you're back in classes again, you've picked up on an anti-American prejudice in many of your professors. No, you aren't imagining it. It's not too complicated to figure out why, though. Nearly all of your professors are Left leaning, and a significant portion of the American Left has cultivated a deep-seated prejudice against their own nation. They fault the United States for offenses they routinely excuse in our nation's enemies. They reject any attempt to celebrate America's founding, take pride in its successes, or argue that America has often stood for noble ideas rather than always pursuing its own naked self-interest. Consider it a hazard of defining yourself by the future ("progressivism"): you tend to depreciate your own past.

But progressives haven't cornered the market on anti-American prejudice. For example, if you squint your eyes and look real hard toward the distant Right, you'll find small and insecure groups of conservatives who exude pathological hatred toward America's minority groups and who wish to rewrite the Constitution to provide for a white ethno-state. As a group, conservatives tend to celebrate our nation's past more often than not. But it's so incredibly modern to despise the past that we shouldn't be surprised to see the sentiment all over the place.

Conservatives and liberals swing the other way, too. Just listen to the way they talk about the United States when their party is in power. Otherwise mute sideliners suddenly become mindless cheerleaders of our nation's government.

The United States isn't perfect, but it isn't in shambles, either. We need to avoid being pathological haters, on the one hand, or mindless cheerleaders, on the other. We should be patriots, men and women who believe in the "ideas" that make us a nation, who love that nation, warts and all. We need to acknowledge with candor the mixed past of what America has been and to work with hope to make America what it should be.

Over the course of the past few months, we've exchanged more than twenty letters, most of which either dealt with the interface of religion and politics in general or religion and hot-button policy issues in specific. Yet, as you noted in your last letter, I haven't engaged in much criticism of the American political arrangement. One reason is that I am grateful for the American experiment; our constitutional arrangement allows significant freedom for religion to flourish, individuals to flourish, society to flourish. I can't think of another nation's constitution under which I'd rather live. Another reason is that the questions you asked ended up taking us in a different direction. But now that you've asked about the dangers of democracy itself . . .

Two especially great temptations plague democracies (or democratic republics) like the United States. The first is that representative democracies display a reflexive urge to confuse the voice of the people (me!) with the voice of God. Our democratic environment can produce warped ideas for both politics and religion. On the religious side, missionary theologian Lesslie Newbigin seems to have read the times right. He notes, "It is perhaps a contemporary manifestation of the general fact of sin that we all have in our heart of hearts the good democratic conviction that God will ultimately bow to public opinion."[1] We humans have always remade God in our own image; these days we simply do it a bit more democratically.

We remake God in our image politically, too, conflating our own voice with God's by making laws that undermine God's most basic norms for human flourishing. Theologian David Wells warns of this temptation when he writes, "For the conforming American, democracy is not simply a political system but an entire worldview, dictating, among many other things, that *culture and truth belong to the people and in a sense are determined by the people.*"[2] When we succumb to this temptation, our democracy (a healthy political arrangement in which people can flourish) lapses into democratism (an idolatrous ideology that undermines human flourishing by undermining God's basic norms). If we assume the majority voice is the good, beautiful, and divine one, we are confusing power with justice. Democratism believes that "might makes right." The order there is backwards.

The other key temptation that plagues a representative democracy like America's is the natural impulse of the majority to place their own interest above the interest of minority groups or individuals. This "tyranny of the majority" is a quick and surefire way to destroy our nation and undermine our pursuit of liberty and justice for all. Most of us recognize this tendency when we are on the short end of the stick. But it's a universal temptation, common on the Left as well as the Right.

On the Left, for instance, there is a hard rump of secular progressives who will not be satisfied until they have systematically dismantled and demonized the historic Christian moral framework that undergirds our nation's Constitution. They tend to obsess on sex and gender and wield those topics as weapons in the culture wars. Many progressives make this claim rather overt.

Yet on the Right there is an equally hard rump of secular conservatives who want to dismantle and demonize the same Christian framework. The difference? They tend to use white cultural heritage as their preferred weapon in the culture wars.

Democracy has enormous potential for good as well as evil. I don't want to see us jettison it because it is difficult or because it has been abused in the past. I want us to harness the good of this system for the good of our neighbors.

To really get the best out of democracy, some changes might be in order. I can think of at least three ways I'd love to see the American experiment adjusted. If given a Magical Political Pen and thirty minutes, this is what I'd do.

First, *I'd clarify the proper approach to constitutional interpretation.* As we discussed in an earlier letter, the United States finds itself in a situation in which a number of Supreme Court justices take a "living document" view of the Constitution. In effect, this view allows an absurdly small number of people to take things out of the Constitution that they do not like and insert things they do. (*Professor Ashford? Isn't that what you just said you were doing with your Magic Pen?* Yes. But my Magic Pen takes an originalist approach to the Constitution. Plus, I don't actually have a Magic Pen.) The prime examples of this sort of activism are the *Roe v. Wade* (1973) and *Obergefell v. Hodges* (2015) rulings, both of which created new "rights" out of thin air. We can guess what else might follow, but the options are nearly endless. Hardly any of them are favorable.

I wish the Founding Fathers had found a way to write the originalist view into the Constitution. They held an originalist view, of course, and had no way of foreseeing a situation in which reasonable Americans would read it in any other way. The threat of reading the Constitution through the lens of postmodern literary theory wasn't on their mind. But it's on ours, so it's up to us, twenty-first-century Americans, to oppose absurd and abusive readings of our founding documents. We must demand that our justices interpret the Constitution the way people living at the time of its adoption would have. The Constitution means what it meant to the ones who ratified it in 1788, or it means nothing at all. If we are able somehow to secure a Court that favors an originalist view, we would no longer have to deal with the specter of nine begowned Ivy League lawyers determining the social and moral course of our nation.

Second, I would *clarify the proper relationship between religion and politics and between church and state.* As I've written to you before, it simply isn't possible to separate religion and politics, but it *is* possible (yea, and desirable) to separate church and state. We humans are incurably religious, whether we cling to religious titles or not. And religion affects politics, without exception. As Richard John Neuhaus never tired of saying, "Politics is chiefly a function of culture, at the heart of culture is morality, and at the heart of morality is religion."

But despite the tight connection between religion and politics, we need to keep an appropriate separation between *church* and *state*. Respect the sanctity of the cultural spheres—their centers and their circumferences—and don't smush them together. Venn Diagrams don't work well in spheres of culture. When the church oversteps her bounds, she fouls up both the church and the government; when the state oversteps its bounds into the ecclesial world, we all end up the poorer for it.

Third, I would *clear a path for the United States to develop multiple major political parties* rather than continuing to put duct tape on the two-party system that is struggling to meet our nation's needs. Political scientist James Skillen has reiterated, over the course of the past several decades, that a number of facets of our American electoral system are aggravating one another into a downward spiral. May I provide another list?

1. Our country has only a single nationally-elected official to represent more than 300 million people.
2. Our major political parties are no longer able to construct national agendas that bind their constituents together for postelection governance. (Can I get a witness?)
3. Political candidates who win elections represent entire districts of people (including large numbers of

people who voted against them) rather than a constituency of citizens who voted for them.

4. Voters feel disconnected from, and usually mistrustful toward, the politicians who supposedly represent them.

5. Elected politicians can and often do function as lone rangers.

6. Elected politicians tend to have their strongest connections with special interest groups rather than with national parties or the supporting voters of their own districts.[3]

It's taken us a while to get to this point, but that combination isn't a winning one. It has produced elected representatives who tend to be special-interest brokers rather than public-interest representatives. It has pushed citizens like you and me either to be uninvolved in politics or, at the other extreme, to throw all of our energy into special-interest pressure games, court litigation, or marches and protest movements. And it has provided an environment that is toxic to mature public-interest debate, the construction of substantive platforms, and policy alternatives. Our political garden is overrun with weeds that we've allowed to grow for generations.

Developing several major political parties wouldn't immediately produce abundant fruit in our political garden, but it would help us uproot many of the weeds. If we had multiple major political parties, Jesus-loving Christians (and other Americans, of course) would have a broader array of options when seeking a political party that better fits our beliefs and values and, as a result, might not feel so politically homeless. We might see political leaders who listened to their constituencies, creating trust in their elected officials again. And it might even help toward lessening the "us versus them" rhetoric of the two-party system—though that spirit would certainly endure.

Unfortunately, I'm not optimistic that we'll have anything other than the choices of Republican or Democrat for the foreseeable future. I won't stop arguing for it, but the inertia there is pretty heavy. But that's OK. If need be, I can live as a politically homeless Christian in our two-party system because we will never find a political platform that fully aligns with the gospel anyway. The more disappointing each of our parties becomes, the less we should be tempted to imbue those parties with messianic hopes. One day we will find our political home when Jesus returns to install a one-party system in which justice will roll down like the waters (Amos 5:24).

Speaking of which, when we go to the Lord or when he returns victorious, we will meet him first and foremost as Christians. But we will also meet him as twenty-first-century Americans. Being American is not the most important aspect of our identity, but it is an inescapable aspect and one for which we will give account. So let's avoid the temptation to be haters or cheerleaders and instead be American Christians who want the best for our nation, putting ourselves at the heart of every good movement of social, cultural, and political concern.

Well, that's all for now. Your most recent letter to me suggested that you also want to talk about (1) your growing disillusionment with American politics and public discourse and (2) how to be a public witness for Christ even when you find yourself in a position of political "weakness." Those are enormously important questions, Christian. I'm glad you asked, and I'm happy to address them in our next couple of exchanges. Let me stew on those, and I'll get back to you.

In the meantime, hit the books. And maybe get some sleep.

Yours,

Bruce

CHAPTER 25

RECOVERING THE LOST ART OF CHRISTIAN PERSUASION

Christian,

It's a pretty big deal that you've been awarded "Junior Writer of the Year" at CCNN in honor of your opinion writing this summer *and* "Most Independent Thinker" for the midterm paper you submitted in your Modern Political Ideologies course. You've taken abuse from both sides of the aisle this past year because of your attempts to carve out a distinctively Christian approach to politics and public life. Hopefully these awards give you a little taste of the satisfaction that comes from sticking to your guns and refusing to conform so easily to ascendant secular political views. You won't always get the awards for working with integrity, compassion, and grit, but it's always worth it.

We've finished discussing your list of hot-button topics. Before I officially sign off, however, I wanted to address a couple of other issues—(1) American conservatism and (2) public witness from the cultural margins. You mentioned both issues in your last letter. Let me tackle that former topic here.

As the savvy reader you are, you've noticed that, although I often criticize aberrant versions of American conservatism, my way of thinking is a conservative way of thinking—at least in terms of the American political spectrum. Based on our conversations during the past year, I can see that you are also a politically conservative Christian. From your perspective, as you put it in your last letter, you are "a bit to the Right" and I'm "center Right." From the perspective of right-wing populists, we're both fake conservatives. From the perspective of left-wingers, we're right-wing crazies.

Let's go ahead and own the conservative label for the time being. If you were so inclined, how might you try to persuade people toward your conservative views?

Let me answer that by reflecting a bit on my up-and-down experience with American conservatism. I discovered the conservative movement when I attended college during the 1990s. I participated in College Republicans, listened to conservative talk-show hosts, and wanted to be actively involved in public life as a conservative.

To make things more interesting, I also became a devoted evangelical Christian during this time. At first I was comfortable with my twin identities of "movement conservative" and "evangelical Christian." I toggled back and forth fairly easily between conservative talk shows on the one hand and my Bible on the other. After all, conservatives promoted family values and religious liberty while fighting against abortion, Soviet Communism, and other evils. I didn't even see them as twin identities because so many people in my circles conflated the two ideas.

Midway through college, however, I became uncomfortable with the uncivil and even caustic demeanor displayed by many conservative radio show hosts, cable TV pundits, and opinion writers. I was uncomfortable because Scripture is clear that we should speak the truth with love and respect for our conversation partners. But many talk-show hosts and pundits urged me by their own example to degrade people on the other side of the political aisle by demonizing them, questioning their motives, and caricaturing their arguments.

I was also uneasy with what seemed to be the calloused attitude some conservatives had toward people who are financially disadvantaged or socially marginalized. I was uneasy because the Bible is packed with directives to care for the poor, be hospitable to people from other ethnic groups, and so forth. I wondered why conservatives didn't care enough for the poor and marginalized to actively show how conservative economic programs will bring more long-term benefit to the poor more than progressive programs will. I'm not sure if this has always been the case, but as I grew up, "compassionate conservatism" started to seem like a contradiction in terms.

Internally, I couldn't reconcile my twin identities. So I just got rid of one of them. I resigned the College Republicans, cast aside my aspirations to be a political journalist, and went into full-time Christian ministry as a missionary, pastor, and seminary professor. I decided I didn't want to play the game anymore.

Fast-forward twenty years. I have reengaged in public life as a professor of public theology and a frequent writer for politically conservative media outlets, and I can see everywhere the negative fruits of the incivility that took root in 1990s conservatism. Conservatives and progressives together have created a toxic political environment in which citizens don't trust each other, our leaders, or our cultural institutions. Citizens more often berate and mock each other than they have serious political discussions. In a context like this, many young Christians are coming to the same disillusioned conclusion I did, walking away from political involvement because the whole game is rotten.

I left political conservatism. But I also came back. As I've spent the lion's share of these letters showing you, I believe conservatives must come together to fix this mess rather than ignoring it or being part of the problem. And that means coming to grips with some uncomfortable truths in the GOP house.

To be sure, a superficial assessment of our current situation might point to the GOP's electoral victories and conclude that movement conservatism is healthy. But consider the fact that the GOP is regularly losing the popular vote, the Hispanic vote, the black vote, the female vote, and the Millennial vote. The majority of our nation rejects the GOP's message.

Even though "conservatism" should by no means be equated with the GOP, I think it safe to say that movement conservatism is weakening at the same rate that the GOP is weakening. This situation will not be easily reversed; every election cycle brings with it millions of new college graduates, the majority of whom are drawn toward progressive ideals.

If conservatism is going to have a vibrant future in our nation, we've got to get better. We will, once again, have to draw upon our better angels by casting aside the temptation to misrepresent, mock, condescend to, or otherwise belittle progressives and progressive views. If we believe the conservative vision for our society is best, then we must put in the hard work to persuade those who lean to the Left. If we do not, we will lose not only future voters but also opportunities to shape America's moral future.

Our ideological opponents are not enemies to be destroyed. They are peers to be persuaded. It reminds me of

Abraham Lincoln's retort to an older woman who was criticizing him for being too soft. She felt that Lincoln wasn't using strong enough rhetoric about the Confederate Southerners, whom she considered irreconcilable enemies who must be destroyed. Lincoln calmly replied, "Why madam, do I not destroy my enemies when I make them my friends?"

We need more of that spirit today. We need not soften our conviction one iota to make this shift. If we fail to do this, the future of conservatism is bleak.

American conservatives have lost the art of persuasion. To allude to two ancient symbols, we've relied too much on the closed fist and not enough on the open hand. I mentioned in a letter a while back that ancient lawyers and experts in rhetoric used the *closed fist* to represent the use of logic, evidence, and argument to give tough and clear answers to those who questioned their beliefs. If we keep Lincoln in mind as our conservative muse, we see that he did this all the time. But the closed fist wasn't his only tactic. He also employed what the ancients symbolized with the *open hand*, representing the combination of creativity, imagination, wit, compassion, and eloquence. He persuaded the hearts and minds of people who were resistant to his ideas. Without that open hand, it is doubtful that he would have won the Civil War. Without a similar open hand today, we won't fare any better.

Let me switch the analogy to drive the point home. Since politically conservative Christians like you are familiar with Christian missions, maybe we can take a page or two out of the playbooks of Christian missionaries. Think about it. A Christian missionary typically moves overseas to minister among a group of people who differ from him linguistically, religiously, socially, culturally, and politically. The missionary's goal is to minister to the people group's needs and to persuade them to consider the claims of Jesus Christ. His tactics are something like the polar opposite of many con-servatives today. He didn't caricature the people group's religion, mock their culture, or impugn their motives.

Instead, a good Christian missionary does three things.

First, a good Christian missionary exhibits genuine con-cern. Christian missionaries move their families overseas at great financial cost, often risking their own lives, for one rea-son: they genuinely care about the people to whom they will minister. They love. Political conservatives must exhibit the same genuine concern—yes, even love—for their ideological foes. If we do not possess such concern, we should quit and go home. Politics should be done out of a desire for the com-mon good, out of service to our fellow citizens. It should be a manifestation of our love for our neighbors. I suspect that, despite our deep flaws, most conservatives really do carry this love around in their hearts. We just need to express it in those terms. We need to take "compassionate conservatism" and show the world that it isn't a contradiction.

Second, good missionaries work hard to find "common ground" with their conversation partners. In other words, they find things upon which they both agree. From that common ground, missionaries find it much easier to per-suade their conversation partners on other matters precisely because they do so from a point of mutual understanding. Don't you know this to be true from your own experience? Who are you more likely to listen to when they challenge you—someone who disagrees with and insults you at every turn (*cough* Uncle John *cough*), or someone who shares many of your convictions?

Third, missionaries take the long view. If conversation partners aren't receptive to their ministry and message, they don't quit and go home. They knew it was going to be a challenge, so they are ready to stick it out for the long haul.

They don't insult their conversation partners' intelligence or impugn their motives. They don't caricature their conversation partners as thoroughly reprehensible people in whom no good can be found. Instead, the missionaries' genuine concern causes them to persevere over the long run. They may end up persuading their conversation partners. They may not. What they won't do is quit because it's hard.

These are the sorts of things American Christians need to do as we seek to persuade other Americans of our vision of the common good. We simply *must* make it clear that compassion drives us. It's worth asking ourselves: *Do we actually care about the people with whom we disagree? Do we want the best for them and for our nation as a whole? Are we doing this to win or because love demands it?*

If we don't ask ourselves these questions, we'll lose. Worse yet, we'll be poor witnesses for Christ. We'll be seen as calloused jerks who are nothing more than the hypocritical and bigoted special interest arm of a major political party. Let's do everything we can so that the charge can't stick.

Comedian Dave Barry summarizes very well the way conservatives are often perceived by the public:

> The Democrats seem to be basically nicer people, but they have demonstrated time and again that they have the management skills of celery. They're the kind of people who'd stop to help you change a flat, but would somehow manage to set your car on fire. I would be reluctant to entrust them with a Cuisinart, let alone the economy. The Republicans, on the other hand, would know how to fix your tire, but they wouldn't bother to stop because they'd want to be on time for Ugly Pants Night at the country club.[1]

Barry's quip may not be the most accurate summary of either political party, but he's got his finger on the pulse of public perception. And perception, while often unfair, doesn't arise from thin air. Why are Democrats considered kind and caring people (even if they can't manage anything)? Why are Republicans considered excellent managers but heartless neighbors? I'll leave the Democrats to grapple with Barry themselves, but I'll admit that for Republicans Barry has shown us the work we have to do. If we continue to get bad press, that's mostly out of our control. But if we don't love our neighbors, that one's on us.

I've been a conservative for many years now. Most of the conservatives I know possess genuine compassion for their neighbors and a positive, uplifting vision for the common good. They became conservatives because they love people. From my conversation with you, Christian, I see the same heart. My encouragement to you is to let your family, neighbors, professors, fellow students, Facebook friends, and opinion-column readers see it. Show them a vision of conservative politics that lifts people up, enriches their lives, and strengthens our society. Show them that what you believe is good and true and beautiful. Show them that it flows from a heart of love. If you can do this, resisting the temptation to become cynical and hardened, behaving like an angry jerk, you might even succeed in persuading other people to your point of view.

Yours,

Bruce

CHAPTER 26

PUBLIC WITNESS FROM
THE POLITICAL MARGINS

Christian,

Yes, I'm happy to help you with the essay you're submitting for the Wilberforce Prize. You mentioned that the essay must address contemporary politics and public life from a distinctively Christian perspective and that you want to reflect on how Christians can be effective public witnesses—even if we approach the public arena from a position of social, cultural, and political weakness.

You've chosen a good topic, one that represents not only your own experience at Dupont University but other Christians' experiences in their communities and workplaces. If the current trajectory of our nation is any indication of what the future holds, Bible-believing Christians will need to equip themselves in this endeavor, learning how to exercise influence without necessarily holding the levers of political power. We've got to learn how to minister from the margins.

As you research and write, you'll need some guides to help you evaluate precisely why and how historic Christianity is getting crowded out in our country. One of your best guides here is the late sociologist Philip Rieff. In his magnum opus, *My Life among the Deathworks*,[1] he argued that the West in general and the United States in particular are in the midst of an unprecedented project to "desacralize" the public square. Or, in ordinary language, to eliminate religion from public life.

Civilizations, Rieff notes, have always understood that their social order is influenced by the sacred order. In other words, what a civilization believes about God and morality (sacred order) will determine how it orders society (social order). Sacred order has always provided a moral code for society and a way of understanding life's meaning. Sacred order shapes a civilization's cultural institutions—such as families, businesses, schools, and governments—in order to shape what a society believes and values. In other words, religion shapes cultural institutions, which in turn shape individuals.

Remember what I said about Richard John Neuhaus a couple of letters back? "Politics is chiefly a function of culture, at the heart of culture is morality, and at the heart of morality is religion." Neuhaus and Rieff are speaking each other's language.

Until now, the West readily acknowledged this intuitive sacred-social connection. For us, Christianity was the primary sacred order that shaped our cultural institutions and our society. Christianity has shaped the beliefs, feelings, and values of every generation in Europe and the United States for centuries. It has provided an overarching vision of the good life and served as a powerful means of opposing social and cultural decadence. These things we love and appreciate in our cultural heritage are, to a great extent, the fruit of Christianity's formative influence.

But now many of our society's most powerful people and institutions are sharpening their axes. They want to undo Christianity's influence throughout society. In a profound departure from our past, many of this era's cultural elite (Rieff calls them "the officer class") want a secular framework upon which we can found our identity, learn our morality, and envision our future.

What did Rieff think of all this? He thought it stunk. He argued that these secular power brokers, while desiring to bring new life, were actually poisoning our cultural institutions and society. In fact, he referred to these desacralized cultural institutions and cultural products as "deathworks." Instead of bringing life and vitality to society, they bring death and decay. Thus far, the casualties include the notion of truth, the institution of marriage, and the definition of male and female.

In response to these death works, Christians may be tempted to rewind the clock in an effort to return to some golden era of the past. But we cannot turn back the clock. Instead, we must move forward in the midst of our moment in American history. If the officer class has chopped down some of our most beautiful "trees," we don't help ourselves out by propping up the dead limbs. We've got to plant new seeds and cultivate new life. It's going to take work, and it's going to take time. But I still believe our country deserves our best efforts at both spiritual and cultural renewal.

So, back to your original question: What does it look like for God's people to speak and act responsibly when we have been decentered? When many Americans consider our doctrines and our ethical framework not only wrong but morally reprehensible? When we are no longer able to catapult politicians into office or bend the ear of legislators who might be able to help align our nation's decrees and laws with an evangelical vision for human flourishing? Can we really minister to our culture from a position of weakness? Can we minister from the margins?

We can, and we must. Instead of resenting our cultural moment, slouching into bitter withdrawal, or charging into angry activism, evangelicals should accept the challenge of our era and serve our nation from a position of weakness. After all, Christian, our Lord ministered from a position of weakness, didn't he? During his earthly ministry, he didn't have social, cultural, or political power. He was decentered and marginalized. Yet, he gave the most powerful public witness of all time.

His first disciples didn't have much going for them, either. They weren't among the cultural elites. They weren't political movers and shakers. To the contrary, they were hunted down and killed almost as soon as the movement got started. And yet, they turned the world upside down.

As his disciples, we can do the same. When the risen Jesus said to the apostles, "As the Father has sent me, I also send you" (John 20:21), he held out his hands to them, affirming that their public witness would also follow the way of the cross.[2]

As the Civil War hymn put it, "As he died to make men holy, let us die to make men free." God's truth marches on through sacrifice and weakness. It didn't make sense to people in the first century, and it won't make sense to people today. But that which was foolishness to the Greeks contains the very wisdom of God. The way of the cross is the way of life.

But what will "the way of the cross" look like to American Christians like you, Christian, who are involved in politics and public life?

For starters, we must renew our commitment to the local church. When the crucified-but-risen Jesus ascended, he left in place a new community: the church. The local church's power is not found in political activism but in preaching the gospel. When we hear the gospel preached and we gather around the Lord's Table, we are being spiritually fortified. We are being prepared to live out our Christianity in our homes, neighborhoods, workplaces, and even the political arena.

The church's gospel preaching challenges the dominant political idols and ideologies of any nation, including the United States. By proclaiming that Jesus is Lord (and Caesar is not), the church nourishes our political identity and previews the day when the Lord will return to usher in a political era marked by justice, peace, and prosperity.

But Sunday morning worship is not an end in itself. Sunday morning worship prepares us for Monday morning public life. If the roots of public Christian goodness are firmly planted in the soil of the church's corporate worship and its missional sending, the public fruits of Christian goodness will be displayed in our neighborhoods, communities, and workplaces. Some may despise the fruit, but we cling to the words of the apostle Paul: "To some we are an aroma of death leading to death, but to others, an aroma of life leading to life" (2 Cor. 2:16). To those building death works, our gospel life will seem repugnant. But life it will remain.

What will it look like to display these fruits, especially in an era when most of our culture's power brokers reject the evangelical vision for the common good? No matter how weak our position is politically, I think we still have four opportunities before us.

First, we need to *reintroduce God to the public imagination*. God is the benevolent cosmic King who designed the universe so that humans can flourish. For the good of our nation, therefore, let's show that the Bible's overarching narrative—rather than a cable news network narrative—is the true story of the whole world. Let's make clear in our personal lives that Jesus—rather than sex, money, or power—is Lord. And let's make clear in our public lives that our ultimate allegiance is to Jesus Christ, not to any particular political ideology, party, or platform. In a world railing against God's authority, any allegiance to his kingly rule will stand out.

Of course, I am not saying we cannot be active in political parties or supportive of political candidates. We can and often we should. But as we engage in politics, we must remember that our political commitments and affiliations are tentative in light of our loyalty to Jesus Christ. Occupants to Caesar's throne come and go; Jesus remains forever.

Second, we need to *decenter ourselves in our political endeavors.* Any attempt to recenter God must be accompanied by a decentering of the self. One way to decenter ourselves is to seek the good of the city (Jer. 29:5–7) rather than merely the good of our own tribe. If we are seeking what's best for our nation as a whole, rather than merely what is best for us as a special interest group, we will be the first to work on behalf of people who are financially disadvantaged, socially marginalized, or downtrodden due to race, ethnicity, or culture. Our love for Christ demands this type of broadminded goodness, and our position of political weakness cannot restrain it.

Another way to decenter ourselves is to be concerned not only with the truth of our moral and political stances but with the way in which we communicate them. As an antidote to the toxic nature of American public discourse, followers of Christ should mirror not only the content of his teaching but the tenor of his life. It is a deep and ugly irony when we purport to represent a gospel of grace but articulate our views in ways that are rude, dishonest, or mean-spirited. As a friend of mine puts it, you really can't serve Jesus with the spirit of Satan.

Third, we need to *reframe public issues in light of the gospel.* The nature of our Christianity—that we give our ultimate allegiance to Christ and subordinate everything else under him—causes us to take a unique perspective on issues. For example, the gospel reframes our approach to *money* by revealing that it is neither our savior nor our security and by causing us to be radically generous to the economically disadvantaged. Our ideological opponents might criticize our political approach to poverty alleviation, but they should never be able to question our personal generosity or our commitment to the financially disadvantaged.

Similarly, the gospel reframes our approach to *power* by causing us—counterintuitively—to serve and empower others while decentering ourselves. We follow a King who assumed his throne by putting aside his power and welcoming death. The allure of power should have no hold on our hearts. Our ideological opponents might criticize our preferred political party for its abuses of power, but they should never be able to question our own use of power.

As Tim Keller often reminds us, this gospel-informed reframing will break the ability of Americans to dismiss the church as a special interest group beholden to any one political party. The church will be able to regain the distinctiveness and clarity *and strength* of her voice by viewing public issues in light of Christ and his gospel. To some, the aroma of death. To others, the aroma of life. But always distinct.

Fourth, we must *revitalize cultural institutions.* We've got to work at renewing cultural realities in such a way that we help shape the instincts and imaginations of future generations. Christ-centered culture work is a powerful means of opposing social and political decadence. You might be surprised how little power you actually need to create life-giving culture. Perhaps you won't transform the entirety of the American political system. But you can build something of cultural beauty and value. Along the way, we'll find that we're also renewing our own marriages, families, churches, and businesses. Aim to bless your neighbors, and you'll find yourself blessed as well.

But be prepared to stick with it. Short-term political activism is a useful tool, but our best building will come by playing the long game and taking the broad view. Don't just make an immediate splash with some hashtag activism. Look beyond what you may be able to accomplish in a week, and work toward what you can accomplish in a decade. Ships turn slowly, but they can turn. And keep your vision broad. Work faithfully to renew *every* dimension and institution of culture, knowing they all feed into each other. You may not be able to anticipate specifically how Christian approaches to art may benefit the family or how Christian influence in education may transform politics. But influence leaks. If Christians are faithfully present in every social sector and cultural institution—every sphere of life—our combined witness will be all the more effective.

So, those are the four opportunities we can seize in our present "weak" position. We take these steps, ultimately, out of obedience to the Lord, rather than in an attempt to win a culture war. Sometimes we will find ourselves having an impact. If so, our efforts will be a preview of his future kingdom. But often we will lose. Death works will win the day. Discouraging as that might be, we should never be dismayed. We don't work to bless our culture in order to win. We do it because we love our Lord and our fellow citizens.

If I were the last Christian in our nation, I'd still faithfully pursue these four opportunities. And I'd do it with a sense of joy and anticipation.

Before I sign off, let me encourage you to keep the faith over the long haul. You'll be pressured to compromise your principles, to take some other path besides the way of the cross. Resist. The way of the cross is *prophetic*. Just as Jesus declared that he is Lord and Caesar is not, so we must challenge the public idols of our own nation. You'll be tempted to focus on your own rights. Resist. The way of the cross is *sacrificial*. Just as Jesus ministered as a homeless itinerant Teacher, we must be willing to serve our nation from a position of weakness rather than power and in the face of disapproval instead of applause. You'll find yourself being seduced by cynicism and pessimism. Resist. The way of the cross is *humbly confident*. As dark as our political moment may seem, the realm of politics will one day be raised to life, made to bow in submission to the King. Since Jesus will gain victory and restore the earth, we remain confident. And since it will be his victory, we remain humble.

We owe it to our nation to be public witnesses from a position of weakness. To paraphrase the apostle Paul's words,

> We Christians have pleaded with God to give us more cultural power. Instead, God has given us a position of weakness. Three times we have pleaded with the Lord that we should regain our power. But he continues to say to us, "My grace is sufficient for you, for my power is made perfect in weakness." Therefore we must boast all the more gladly in our political weaknesses, so that the power of Christ may rest upon us. For the sake of Christ, then, we are content with political weakness, with cultural obscurity, with

social smallness, with uphill battles and the threat of defeat. For when we are weak, then we are strong. (2 Cor. 12:7–10)

Yours,
Bruce

ABOUT THE AUTHOR

Bruce Ashford is provost and professor of theology and culture at Southeastern Baptist Theological Seminary. He is the author or coauthor of *One Nation Under God: A Christian Hope for American Politics* (B&H, 2015), *Every Square Inch: An Introduction to Cultural Engagement for Christians* (Lexham, 2015), and *I Am Going* (B&H, 2016). He is married to Lauren, with whom he has two daughters and a son.

He has been featured in *Fox News Opinion, First Things Magazine, USA Today, The Daily Signal, The Daily Caller, The Gospel Coalition*, and other national outlets. He has appeared on National Public Radio (NPR), the *Eric Metaxas Show*, the *Pat Williams Show, In the Market with Janet Parshall, Janet Mefferd Today, Chris Fabry Live!*, and other nationally syndicated shows.

He is a senior fellow in public theology at the Kirby Laing Institute for Christian Ethics (Cambridge, United Kingdom), a participant in the Dulles Colloquium of the Institute on Religion and Public Life (New York, New York), and a research fellow at the Ethics and Religious Liberty Commission (Nashville, Tennessee).

He has spoken at universities, seminaries, and churches across Europe, Africa, Asia, and the Middle East, including those associated with the Baptist, Presbyterian, Anglican, Methodist, and Assemblies of God denominations.

NOTES

Chapter 1

1. Thomas Haliburton, *Letter-Bag of the Great Western: Or, Life in a Steamer* (Paris: Baudry's European Library, 1840), 100.

2. John Rawls, *A Theory of Justice*, rev. ed. (Cambridge, MA: Belknap Press of Harvard University, 1999); Rawls, *Justice as Fairness* (Cambridge, MA: Belknap Press of Harvard University, 2001).

3. John Rawls, *Political Liberalism,* exp. ed. (New York: Columbia University Press, 2005).

4. G. K. Chesterton, "Orthodoxy," in *The Collected Works of G. K. Chesterton*, ed. David Dooley, vol. 1: *Heretics, Orthodoxy, and The Blatchford Controversies* (San Francisco: Ignatius Press, 1986), 270.

Chapter 2

1. In polite company the phrase "oldest profession" has often been used as an indirect way of referring to prostitution.

2. Bruce Riley Ashford and Chris Pappalardo, *One Nation Under God: A Christian Hope for American Politics* (Nashville: B&H Academic, 2015), 7–8.

3. The terms *structural* and *directional* are terms contemporary theologians use to describe the tension between good and evil in the various spheres of life. See Al Wolters, *Creation Regained: Biblical Basics for a Reformational Worldview*, 2nd ed. (Grand Rapids, MI: Eerdmans, 2005), 87–114.

4. Ashford and Pappalardo, *One Nation Under God,* 11.

Chapter 3

1. John Dickson, *The Best Kept Secret of Christian Mission: Promoting the Gospel with More Than Our Lips* (Grand Rapids, MI: Zondervan, 2013), 115–23.

Chapter 4

1. C. S. Lewis, "Answers to Questions on Christianity," in *God in the Dock* (Grand Rapids, MI: Eerdmans, 2014), 36.

Chapter 5

1. N. T. Wright, "The New Testament and the State," *Themelios* 16.1 (1990): 12–13.

Chapter 8

1. Balthasar Hübmaier, *On Heretics and Those Who Burn Them,* in *Balthasar Hübmaier: Theologian of Anabaptism*, trans. and ed. H. Wayne Pipkin and John H. Yoder (Scottsdale, PA: Herald, 1989), 60.

2. "Peaceful Coexistence: Reconciling Nondiscrimination Principles with Civil Liberties," Washington, DC: U.S. Commission on Civil Rights, September 7, 2016, http://www.usccr.gov/pubs/Peaceful-Coexistence-09-07-16.PDF.

3. William Saletan, "Purge the Bigots: Brendan Eich Is Just the Beginning. Let's Oust Everyone Who Donated to the Campaign Against Gay Marriage," *Slate*, April 4, 2014, http://www.slate.com/articles/news_and_politics/frame_game/2014/04/brendan_eich_quits_mozilla_let_s_purge_all_the_antigay_donors_to_prop_8.html.

Chapter 9

1. Michael Bloomberg and Charles Koch, "Why Free Speech Matters on Campus: 'Safe Spaces' Will Create Graduates Unwilling to Tolerate Differing Opinions—a Crisis for a Free Society," *The Wall Street Journal*, May 12, 2016, http://www.wsj.com/articles/why-free-speech-matters-on-campus-1463093280.

2. Eugene Volokh, "At the University of Oregon, No More Free Speech for Professors on Subjects Such as Race, Religion, Sexual Orientation," *The Washington Post*, December 26, 2016,

https://www.washingtonpost.com/news/volokh-conspiracy/wp
/2016/12/26/at-the-university-of-oregon-no-more-free-speech-for-
professors-on-subjects-such-as-race-religion-sexual-orientation/.

3. Susan Svrluga, "Don't Ask Us for Trigger Warnings or Safe
Spaces, the University of Chicago Tells Freshmen," *The Washington
Post*, August 25, 2016, https://www.washingtonpost.com/news/
grade-point/wp/2016/08/25/dont-ask-us-for-trigger-warnings-or-
safe-spaces-the-university-of-chicago-tells-freshmen/.

Chapter 10

1.*Merriam-Webster Dictionary, s.v.* "embryo," accessed August
15, 2017, https://www.merriam-webster.com/dictionary/embryo/;
Merriam-Webster Dictionary, s.v. "fetus," accessed August 15, 2017,
https://www.merriam-webster.com/dictionary/fetus.

2. Judith Jarvis Thompson, "A Defense of Abortion," *Philosophy
& Public Affairs*, vol. 1, no. 1 (Fall 1971). Accessed from http://spot.
colorado.edu/~heathwoo/Phil160,Fall02/thomson.htm.

3. "Personalty," The Free Dictionary, http://legal-dictionary.
thefreedictionary.com/personalty.

4. Scott Klusendorf, *The Case for Life* (Wheaton: Crossway,
2009), 28–29.

5. If you want to learn more, you can see a more exten-
sive list (of twenty-six) in "The America We Seek: A Statement
of Pro-Life Principle and Concern," *First Things*, no. 63 (May
1996): 40–44, accessed August 15, 2016, https://www.firstthings.
com/article/1996/05/005-the-america-we-seek-a-statement-of-pro-
life-principle-and-concern.

6. Mary Ann Glendon, "The Women of *Roe v. Wade*," *First
Things* 134 (June 2003): 19–23, accessed August 15, 2017, https://
www.firstthings.com/article/2003/06/the-women-of-roe-v-wade.

Chapter 11

1. George Yancey, *Beyond Racial Gridlock: Embracing Mutual
Responsibility* (Downers Grove: InterVarsity, 2006), 29–74.

2. Mika Edmondson, "Is Black Lives Matter the New Civil
Rights Movement?," *The Gospel Coalition*, June 24, 2016, https://
www.thegospelcoalition.org/article/is-black-lives-matter-the
-new-civil-rights-movement.

3. Anthony Bradley, "Black Lives Matter Doesn't Represent the Gospel, nor Should It," *World Magazine*, January 15, 2016, https://world.wng.org/2016/01/black_lives_matter_doesnt_represent_the_gospel_nor_should_it.

4. Edmondson, "Is Black Lives Matter the New Civil Rights Movement?"

5. Edmondson, "Is Black Lives Matter the New Civil Rights Movement?"

6. Jason L. Riley, "A Better Direction for Black Lives Matter," *The Wall Street Journal*, June 27, 2017, https://www.wsj.com/articles/a-better-direction-for-black-lives-matter-1498604674.

Chapter 12

1. "I Disapprove of What You Say, but I Will Defend to the Death Your Right to Say It." Quote Investigator, accessed August 24, 2017, https://quoteinvestigator.com/2015/06/01/defend-say.

2. Ben R. Crenshaw, "Shut Up, Bigot!: The Intolerance of Tolerance," *Public Discourse*, August 12, 2015, accessed August 24, 2017, http://www.thepublicdiscourse.com/2015/08/15398.

3. Angelo M. Codevilla, "The Rise of Political Correctness," *Claremont Review of Books*, November 8, 2016, accessed August 24, 2017, http://www.independent.org/printer.asp?page=%2Fnewsroom%2Farticle%2Easp?id=8932.

4. William Deresiewicz, "On Political Correctness," *The American Scholar*, March 6, 2017, accessed August 24, 2017, https://theamericanscholar.org/on-political-correctness.

5. Ibid.

6. Richard Mouw, *Uncommon Decency: Christian Civility in an Uncivil World* (Downers Grove, IL: IVP Books, 2010), 14.

Chapter 13

1. Brian Fikkert and Steve Corbett, *When Helping Hurts: Alleviating Poverty without Hurting the Poor . . . and Yourself* (Chicago, IL: Moody Publishers, 2009), 62.

2. Ray Dalio, "Economic Principles," in *Economic Principles: How the Economic Machine Works,* August 7, 2017, http://www.economicprinciples.org/wp-content/uploads/ray_dalio__how_the_economic_machine_works__leveragings_and_deleveragings.pdf.

3. Don Boudreaux, "Everything Has Its Price (and That's a Good Thing)," *Learn Liberty*, June 15, 2015, http://www.learn liberty.org/videos/everything-has-its-price-and-thats-a-good-thing/.

4. Jay W. Richards, "Why Good Intentions Aren't Good Enough" (presented at the The Wisdom Forum, Southeastern Baptist Theological Seminary, March 15, 2015), http://intersectproject. org/faith-and-economics/jay-richards-why-good-intentions-arent -good-enough/.

Chapter 14

1. Randy E. Barnett and Blackman, *Constitutional Law: Cases in Context, 2017 Supplement*, 2nd ed. (New York: Wolters Kluwer, 2017), 202.

2. Ibid., 200.

3. Christians might read my criticisms of the living document approach and think, "But the Bible says it is 'living and breathing.' So how is the Bible not a living document, and why doesn't that imply we should take a 'living document' approach to interpreting it?" And that is a good question. The big difference is in how we define *living*. Whereas in the legal realm, a "living" document view is one that allows the reader to reinterpret the original meaning of the text, in the theological realm, the Bible is "living" in the sense that the living God works through the original meaning of the Bible's text to do his good will in our lives.

4. Antonin Scalia, "Mullahs of the West: Judges as Moral Arbiters" (presented at the Annual Meeting of the North Carolina Bar Association, Asheville, NC, June 21, 2013), https://www.rpo. gov.pl/pliki/12537879280.pdf.

Chapter 15

1. For a history the use of *U.S. v. Miller* as case law in the subsequent decades, see "Gun Control," *Current Issues: Macmillan Social Science Library*, Opposing Views in Context (Detroit: Gale, 2010), http://link.galegroup.com/apps/doc/PC3021900077/ OVIC?u=sand55832&xid=0e1dc859.

2. Veronica Rose, "Summary of *D.C. v. Heller*," *Connecticut General Assembly*, October 17, 2008, https://www.cga.ct.gov/2008/ rpt/2008-R-0578.htm.

3. John Lott, *More Guns, Less Crime*, 3rd ed. (Chicago: University of Chicago, 2010); Helena Bachmann, "The Swiss Difference: A Gun Culture That Works," *Time*, December 20, 2012, http://world.time.com/2012/12/20/the-swiss-difference-a-gun-culture-that-work/.

Chapter 16

1. "Mark Cuban on Trump Administration, Future of Jobs," *Bloomberg.com*, February 17, 2017, https://www.bloomberg.com/news/videos/2017-02-17/mark-cuban-on-trump-administration-future-of-jobs.

2. Northrop Frye, *Nothrop Frye on Religion*, ed. Alvin A. Lee and Jean O'Grady, Collected Works of Northrop Frye (Toronto: University of Toronto Press, 2000), 4.

3. David Hume, "Of the Standard of Taste," in *Essays: Moral, Political, and Literary*, ed. Eugene F. Miller (Indianapolis, IN: Liberty Classics, 1987), 233.

4. Mortimer J. Adler and Charles Van Doren, *How to Read a Book: The Classic Guide to Intelligent Reading* (New York: Touchstone, 2014).

5. T. S. Eliot, "Religion and Literature," as reprinted in Leland Ryken, ed., *The Christian Imagination: The Practice of Faith in Literature and Writing*, rev. and exp. ed. (Colorado Springs, CO: Shaw Books, 2002), 197, 207.

Chapter 17

1. Scott B. Rae, *Moral Choices: An Introduction to Ethics*, 3rd ed. (Grand Rapids, MI: Zondervan, 2009), 284.

2. "Category mistake," *Oxford English Dictionary*, n.d., https://en.oxforddictionaries.com/definition/category_mistake.

3. "Obergefell v. Hodges," *Oyez*, 2015, https://www.oyez.org/cases/2014/14-556.

4. NEED SOURCE INFORMATION Justice Kennedy Obergefell Majority Opinion

5. "Obergefell v. Hodges," *Justia Law*, 2015, https://supreme.justia.com/cases/federal/us/576/14-556/dissent4.html.

6. "Obergefell v. Hodges," *Justia Law*, 2015, https://supreme.justia.com/cases/federal/us/576/14-556/dissent5.html.

7. Richard John Neuhaus, "The Culture Wars Go International," *First Things,* January 2004, https://www.firstthings.com/article/2004/01/the-culture-wars-go-international.

8. Russell Moore, "The Sexual Revolution's Coming Refugee Crisis," July 7, 2015, accessed September 8, 2107, http://www.russellmoore.com/2015/07/07/the-sexual-revolutions-coming-refugee-crisis/.

Chapter 18

1. C. S. Lewis, "Rejoinder to Dr. Pittenger," in *God in the Dock: Essays on Theology and Ethics,* ed. Walter Hooper (Grand Rapids, MI: Eerdmans, 1970), 197.

2. Sarah Cairoli, "Differences between Ecocentric & Biocentric," *Sciencing,* April 25, 2017, http://sciencing.com/differences-between-ecocentric-biocentric-18072.html.

3. Parts of this section have been adapted from Joe Carter's "Shave a Yak, Save a Planet: How to Choose a Climate Change Policy," *Acton Institute PowerBlog,* April 22, 2016, http://blog.acton.org/archives/86363-shave-a-yak-save-a-planet-how-to-choose-a-climate-change-policy.html.

4. Jeremy H. Brown, "Yak Shaving," *MIT Computer Science and Artificial Intelligence Laboratory,* February 11, 2000, http://projects.csail.mit.edu/gsb/old-archive/gsb-archive/gsb2000-02-11.html.

5. "Global Warming and Hurricanes: An Overview of Current Research Results," Text, *Geophysical Fluid Dynamics Laboratory,* March 17, 2017, https://www.gfdl.noaa.gov/global-warming-and-hurricanes/.

6. Carter, "Shave a Yak, Save a Planet."

Chapter 19

1. Catherine E. Shoichet and Azadeh Ansari, "'Sanctuary Campus' Protests Target Trump Immigration Policies," *CNN,* November 16, 2016, http://www.cnn.com/2016/11/16/politics/sanctuary-campus-protests/index.html.

2. Barney Jopson, "Latino Groups Argue Trump's Immigration Stance Close to Obama's," *Financial Times,* November 14, 2016, https://www.ft.com/content/af3454e4-aa91-11e6-ba7d-76378e4fef24.

3. "Fox News Poll," *Fox News*, August 31, 2016, https://fnn.app. box.com/s/mvgz0vr7hux1q4886uro3pyx2tp2wexa.

Chapter 20

1. Bruce Riley Ashford, "Can a Faithful Evangelical Be a Political Nationalist?," *BruceAshford.net*, March 14, 2017, http://bruceashford.net/2017/can-a-faithful-evangelical-be-a-political-nationalist/.

2. G. K. Chesterton, "Orthodoxy," in *The Collected Works of G. K. Chesterton*, ed. David Dooley, vol. 1: *Heretics, Orthodoxy, and The Blatchford Controversies* (San Francisco: Ignatius Press, 1986), 270.

3. C. J. Ciaramella, "Some Well-Dressed White Nationalists Gathered in DC Last Weekend," *Vice*, October 29, 2013, https:// www.vice.com/en_us/article/kwpadw/some-well-dressed-white-nationalists-gathered-in-dc-last-weekend.

4. Ashford, "Can a Faithful Evangelical Be a Political Nationalist?"

5. David T. Koyzis, *Political Visions & Illusions: A Survey & Christian Critique of Contemporary Ideologies* (Downers Grove, IL: InterVarsity Press, 2009), 115.

6. Christopher Caldwell, "The Migrants of Calais: Losers and Winners in the Global Economy," *Weekly Standard*, March 7, 2016, http://www.weeklystandard.com/the-migrants-of-calais/article/2001284; R. R. Reno, "Homeless," *First Things*, June 2016, https://www.firstthings.com/article/2016/06/homeless.

7. David Brooks, "The Coming Political Realignment," *New York Times*, July 1, 2016, sec. Opinion, https://www.nytimes.com/2016/07/01/opinion/the-coming-political-realignment.html.

Chapter 21

1. For Heimbach's *"jus ad bellum"* and *"jus in bello"* criteria, as well as his memo to President George H. W. Bush assessing the justice of invading Iraq in the lead up to the Persian Gulf War, see "The Bush Just War Doctrine: Genesis and Application of the President's Moral Leadership in the Persian Gulf War," in *From Cold War to New World Order: The Foreign Policy of George H. W. Bush*, ed. Meena Rose and Rosanna Perotti (Westport, CT: Greenwood, 2002), 441–64.

2. *U.S. News & World Report*, vol. 110, no. 5 (1991 Feb 11), 32.

Chapter 22

1. Laura Meyers, "Transgender MMA Fighter Destroys Female Opponent," *The Libertarian Republic*, June 10, 2015, http://the-libertarianrepublic.com/transgender-mma-fighter-destroys-female-opponent/.

2. Andrew T. Walker, *God and the Transgender Debate: What Does the Bible Actually Say About Gender Identity?* (Epsom, UK: The Good Book Company, 2017), 94–105.

3. Vaughan Roberts, *Transgender*, Talking Points (Epsom, UK: The Good Book Company, 2016), 37.

4. Paul W. Hruz, Lawrence S. Mayer, and Paul R. McHugh, "Growing Pains: Problems with Puberty Suppression in Treating Gender Dysphoria," *The New Atlantis*, no. 52 (Spring 2017): 27.

5. Andrew T. Walker, "Puberty Suppression and the Transgender Movement: Why Christians Ought to Have Concern," *The Ethics and Religious Liberty Commission of the Southern Baptist Convention,* June 23, 2017, http://erlc.com/resource-library/articles/puberty-suppression-and-the-transgender-movement-why-christians-ought-to-have-concern.

Chapter 23

1. Craig Timberg, "Russian Propaganda Effort Helped Spread 'Fake News' During Election, Experts Say," *Washington Post*, November 24, 2016, https://www.washingtonpost.com/business/economy/russian-propaganda-effort-helped-spread-fake-news-during-election-experts-say/2016/11/24/793903b6-8a40-4ca9-b712-716af66098fe_story.html.

2. Jason Horowitz, "Spread of Fake News Provokes Anxiety in Italy," *New York Times*, December 2, 2016, https://www.nytimes.com/2016/12/02/world/europe/italy-fake-news.html.

3. Andrew Higgins, "It's France's Turn to Worry about Election Meddling by Russia," *New York Times*, April 17, 2017, https://www.nytimes.com/2017/04/17/world/europe/french-election-russia.html.

4. Facebook Security, "Improvements in Protecting the Integrity of Activity on Facebook," *Facebook*, April 12, 2017, https://www.facebook.com/notes/facebook-security/improvements

-in-protecting-the-integrity-of-activity-on-facebook/
10154323366590766.

5. Ira Glass, "599: Seriously?: Act One: Lies Become the Truth," *This American Life*, October 21, 2016, https://www.thisamerican-life.org/radio-archives/episode/599/seriously?act=1.

6. Barney Jopson, "Latino Groups Argue Trump's Immigration Stance Close to Obama's," *Financial Times*, November 14, 2016, https://www.ft.com/content/af3454e4-aa91-11e6-ba7d-76378e4fef24.

7. Ibid.

8. "Oxford Dictionaries Word of the Year 2016 Is . . . ," *Oxford Dictionaries*, November 17, 2016, https://www.oxforddictionaries.com/press/news/2016/11/17/WOTY-16.

9. Ravi Zacharias, "Why Oxford Dictionary's 2016 Word of the Year Matters," *The Gospel Coalition*, December 21, 2016, https://www.thegospelcoalition.org/article/why-oxford-dictionarys-2016-word-of-the-year-matters.

10. Petra McGillen, "How the Techniques of 19th-Century Fake News Tell Us Why We Fall for It Today," *Nieman Lab*, April 11, 2017, http://www.niemanlab.org/2017/04/how-the-techniques-of-19th-century-fake-news-tell-us-why-we-fall-for-it-today/.

11. Eugene Kiley and Lori Robertson, "How to Spot Fake News," *FactCheck.org*, November 18, 2016, http://www.factcheck.org/2016/11/how-to-spot-fake-news/.

12. Peter Stockland, "Journalism, War Crimes, and the Common Good," *Comment Magazine*, June 23, 2011, https://www.cardus.ca/comment/article/2835/journalism-war-crimes-and-the-common-good/.

Chapter 24

1. Lesslie Newbigin, *A Faith for This One World?* (Eugene, OR: Wipf and Stock, 1961), 69.

2. David F. Wells, *God in the Wasteland: The Reality of Truth in a World of Fading Dreams* (Grand Rapids, MI: Eerdmans, 1995), 56. Emphasis added.

3. James W. Skillen, *Recharging the American Experiment: Principled Pluralism for Genuine Civic Community* (Grand Rapids, MI: Baker, 1994).

Chapter 25

1. Dave Barry, *Dave Barry Turns Forty* (New York: Ballantine, 1990), 124.

Chapter 26

1. Philip Rieff, *My Life among the Deathworks: Illustrations of the Aesthetics of Authority* (Charlottesville, VA: University of Virginia Press, 2006).

2. Lesslie Newbigin, *Signs Amid the Rubble* (Eerdmans, 2003), 100.